LIND

and the Bog W   s

Peat train, Lindow Moss, December 1996
courtesy Bridie Feeney

MATTHEW HYDE

and

CHRISTINE PEMBERTON

REX PUBLISHING
2002

REX PUBLISHING

First Floor
The Rex Buildings
Alderley Road
Wilmslow
Cheshire SK9 1HY
Tel. 0845 0909102   Fax. 01625 530900

© Matthew Hyde & Christine Pemberton
ISBN 0 9540391 1 4

Cover design, layout and typesetting
Christine Pemberton

CONTENTS

ACKNOWLEDGEMENTS

During the course of our research many local people have welcomed us into their homes and shared their knowledge and their personal memories with us. Their enthusiasm and participation have greatly enriched this record of Lindow. We would like to thank the following:

Ernest Acton, Maurice Acton, Margaret & the late Bill Arnison, Rosemary Barber, Norma & Roy Barker, Cyril Bradley, Mabel Brighouse, Richard Brown, Jim & Fred Burgess, Minnie & Derek Clarke, Nancy Crook, Anita & Ralph Croxall, John Davies, Sue Dyer, Alex & Richard Ellison, Rene Eckert , Tony Evans, Bridie Feeney, Rev Mel Gray, Robert Hope, Velson Horie, Drs Barbara & Kenneth Howe, Basil Jeuda, Lyn & Howard Joseph, Dave Kitching, Judy & Alan Lane, Rachel & John Mameluk, Jeremy Milln, Alan Mould, Betty & Bruce Mould, Mary & Walter Munnerley, Jenny & Stuart Nixon, Marion & Ken Oldham, Mary Payne, Cynthia & George Potts, Hawthorn James Price, Betty Richardson, Gladys Rogers-Jones, Jim Shepherd, John Spawton, Howard Staves, Lucy & Mike Thomas, Thomas Ward, Janet & Dick White, Bill Whittaker, Stella Willett, Cyril Wood, Eric Worsley.

In addition our thanks to
North West Film Archive
Andrea & Nichola of P Williams
Taffy Davies and Phil Wattis
The staff of the Reference Library, Wilmslow
Graham Walker of the Wilmslow Historical Society

1
Lindow Moss

Lindow Moss

Lindow Moss, mainly a raised peat bog with some large tracts of sand, once encompassed the Hough, Fulshaw, Morley and Chorley, all within the parish of Wilmslow; Great Warford, which falls in the parish of Alderley, plus a large section within the parish of Mobberley.

The original extent of the ancient moss was about 1,500 acres. By 1850 it is recorded as having shrunk by half and by the 1880s only one quarter remained. Even at that time local geologists, naturalists and historians were decrying its exploitation and predicting its demise. What, one wonders, would they have to say if they could see it today? Desecrated, exploited and abused.

At the present time what does survive of the peat bog lies stripped of its dignity. Naked and exposed like a skinned rabbit, there is something shocking about its vulnerability. An uncomfortable feeling that we are looking at something which we were never meant to see.

Modern methods of extraction incorporate surface shredding. In recent months, due to this pulverisation, the area has taken on the appearance of a vast, flat, freshly ploughed field. During the course of many months of research into the past, present and future of Lindow Moss, "That's better. It's looking a lot tidier now!" was the only misguided comment we heard in praise of the current state of play.

And yet, by some miracle, the bog still retains its *Deus loci*, that esoteric essence, the spirit of a place. Peat bogs are mysterious and elemental, ruled by air, earth, fire and water.

Lindow's peat bog, especially that tiny slice which has remained relatively untouched, until now, by the peat extractors, still has that indefinable quality, the capacity to exert a strange and ancient pull. There is a sense of unease and sadness on a bad day, but in the summertime this is replaced by an almost hypnotic feeling of relaxation, lulling one into the desire to sit and ruminate amongst the heather and bilberry bushes, dozing in the warm sunlight.

In late April 2002, just after St Patrick's day, the main north to south ditch, still undisturbed at that time, was covered in thick floating blankets of nitrous green Sphagnum moss; blazing emerald sponges, glowing in the late afternoon sunlight. Soon that final section, along with its sundews and cotton grass, will also be destroyed for ever. What time did to the people, people are now doing to the bog itself.

Lindow Moss owes its genesis to the the last Ice Age, when great glacial sheets from the Pennines pounded the surrounding land with such force that the rocks were reduced to frozen masses of gravel, sand and

Opposite: Battery Lane, now Rotherwood Road, 1990

clay. As temperatures gradually rose the huge floes began to thaw. The melting ice carried these deposits down onto the Cheshire plain and formed wetlands. The lying water was gradually colonised by primitive forms of plant life - algae, water weeds, sedges and Sphagnum mosses. Eventually the peat began to form, which supported more sophisticated plants; rushes, ferns, alder and willow.

Over the centuries the peat levels continued to rise until it was capable of supporting pines and oaks. By the Middle Bronze Age, the area had became forest. Lack of light and the shedding of leaves and pine needles killed off the undergrowth and choked the water courses, which eventually contributed to the destruction of the trees. As the forest died and fell it left in its wake a shallow, stagnant lake. This was the beginning of the formation of the bog. The sedge and sphagnum returned and black peat began to surface, playing host to other bog plants. It became a desolate, treacherous place, feeding off its vegetable, animal and sometimes human victims. Century by century the bog rose and quaked and took possession.

The Early Settlers

The earliest inhabitants would have been the Ancient Britons. Flints have been found around Saltersley which must have been brought from elsewhere, because flints do not occur in this area.

In 1879 astonishing Palæolithic wall paintings were discovered in the Altamira Cave, near the Spanish village of Santillana del Mar in Santander province. The news of this discovery must have excited the Victorian gentlemen scholars of the day, held in thrall as they were with the Darwinian debates on the origins of the species. In 1884, only five years after the discovery of the cave paintings we find William Norbury, who lived on Moor Lane, just a short walk from the peat bog, delivering a lecture to the Lancashire & Cheshire Archeological Society. His chosen subject was "Lindow Common as a Peat Bog - Its Age and Its People".

The cave art must have aroused his interest and directed his attentions towards the Euskarians, the original Basque people thought to be direct descendants of the Stone Age hunters of Altamira. The Basque language - Euskara - appears to be unrelated to any other language on earth. It is still spoken by about half a million people in Northern Spain and SW France, around the area of the Bay of Biscay (Basque Bay), and is now accepted as a regional language. This is all about cultural identity and is of central importance to the Basque Nationalist Movement, rather like the Welsh language is to Wales.

Obviously greatly impressed by what he had read, Norbury makes a giant leap of the imagination and posits the claim that the original inhabitants of Lindow - the ancient Britons- were Euskarian Stone Agers and that those who now lived around these marginal, unwanted lands were their descendants;

"Before closing my paper I will add a few remarks on the peculiar race of people who, until recently, dwelt on the verges of these old commons. From actual observation of their physical characteristics and habits during the last fifty years, I am of opinion that they are of a very ancient race, totally different from the surrounding people. The physical peculiarities are very marked. They have the long head (Dolicho-cephalic), projecting eyebrows, high cheek bones, strong and coarse limbs, leaden aspect, slow motions, and, in a very marked degree, the Moorish skin - the colour of the skin very like the gipsy's, but very unlike in every other feature. Their habits and modes of life in the early part of the present century were peculiar. They were often buck-stealers, poachers, and fishers, the transmitted instincts of the chase having come down with them through the ages. This would lead them to the commons and most neglected parts of the country. Their callings and handicrafts also seem to point to their being of a primitive people who have kept their ancient habits. They are expert in using twigs or osiers, in making besoms from birch and broom, also in making straw-work, beehives, &c., from split briars and straw, and they are very expert in making primitive traps and snares from withies and bands; in fact, in using all kinds of natural and ready products of the country. Those who kept animals had the most primitive kinds, as dogs, pigs, geese, and ducks, but especially asses, for carrying their baskets and brooms to where they could sell them.

They were very sly and very suspicious, as aboriginal races are always; apparently very harmless, but not so safe as they appeared to be. When exasperated they would fight with anything that lay next them - bills, spades, pikels, swipples, or any of their rude implements, and with these they were, as they say in their vernacular, "lungeous." Some of the fiercer kind, if close pressed, would fight with their mouths, and bite like bulldogs. I may add that they in a general way shunned society, and appeared to be almost destitute of religious instincts."

The vanquished and enslaved Euskarians learned to speak the dialect of their Celtic lords as they afterwards learned to speak that of their Roman conquerors.

But from the ethnological point of view a Euskarian is a Euskarian still, whatever language he may happen to speak. His tongue would produce no immediate change in the colour of his skin and eyes. To this day the darker people are mainly to be found among the peasantry. And, I might add, especially on the borders of commons and mosses.

Let anyone who is acquainted with the different localities, and who can remember fifty years back, recall the kind of people there were on Lindow Common, Sale Moor, Heyhead, Lifeless Moss, Mottram Common, Broken Cross,

Rudheath, and Biddulph Moor, and I think I might add Southport - whose donkey drivers and sand-grounders are from the end of a bog at Churchtown, and who were there before Southport was built - and I think he will arrive at the fact that these different peoples were until recently of a distinct race from the people of the rest of the country; that they were, in fact, of the old Euskarian race, driven to these bogs long ages before the Romans set foot in Britain.

At first they fled to these 'dismal swamps' from the face of the conquering peoples, and lived outside of civilisation in their own primitive way for long ages. In later times there is a legal reason for their continuing upon these bogs. After the breaking up of the feudal system and serfdom came the Poor Law, with its law of settlement. "Whereas by reason of some defects in the law, poor people are not restrained from going from one parish to another, and therefore do endeavour to settle themselves in those parishes where there is the best stock, the largest commons or wastes to build cottages, and the most woods for them to burn and destroy," provides "that upon complaint made to any justice of the peace, within forty days after such person coming to settle, or who coming to inhabit is likely to be chargeable, such justices shall by their warrant convey such person to such parish where he was last legally settled, either as a native, householder, sojourner, apprentice, or servant."

If such person returned after removal, he was summarily convicted as a vagabond and sent to prison - and this whether he troubled the parish or not. After a time this law was somewhat ameliorated in its incidence (though it yet disgraces our statute-book) and then a man could remain anywhere provided he asked for nothing; but if when in poverty he asked for help, the old inhuman law laid hold of him and took him to his old place, so that this law of settlement would have a strong action in keeping these ancient people to their old haunts.

Improved legislation in the direction of freedom helped to absorb these people to a great extent in the surrounding populations: but the final agent in almost obliterating the distinctive races of these old people about our mosses was the spread of education and religion among the common people*, first done by the Sunday schools of the latter part of the last century and the earlier part of this century. The old parish churches were far distant, and in the best parts and heart of the parishes; but upon Sunday schools being established around the commons, the commoners' children were gathered with the farmers' and labourers' children of the locality: intermarriages followed, and eventually almost all traces of our ancient commoner - the ancient Euskarian - have disappeared, and will, ere long, disappear entirely and for ever."

* See 'Civilising the Bog Dwellers'.

The Celts

.. in the face of the sun, in the eye of the light and the expansive freedom of the sky." Julo MSS p432

A description of the assembly sites chosen for outdoor gatherings and Bardic (Druidic) worship. They gathered to worship the sun, the moon and the planets. Their mortal ruler was the Priest, but only with the sanction of the Otherworld.

During the Iron Age small groups of people began to settle around the drier sandy areas at the margins. To begin to understand this early pastoral population, one has to realise that existence was a fragile thing. The earth was the mother who succoured them, holding the power of life and death. This was a time when people respected and revered their land.

The Celts were taught that bogs and lakes and all watery places were entrances to the Otherworld. The deep pools created within that treacherous terrain were gateways to the abode of their gods and goddesses and the raised peat bog was held sacred. They gave great ceremonial thanks, accompanied by votive offerings and blood sacrifices cast into dark waters to appease and placate.

As a small child I was frequently warned off pools and streams by both my Welsh grandmother and my aunt. 'Don't peer over the edge.' they frequently cautioned. "Jinny Greenteeth will get you." I believed them, and always kept well back, having no wish to encounter the terrible green hag who lurked beneath the water weeds. Interestingly, a Djinn, or Djinnee, belongs to Moslem demonology. It is an evil spirit possessing supernatural powers and capable of appearing in both human and animal form to take possession of the unwary.

They made a huge effort for the great calendar festivals - the summer and winter solstices, and four ritual celebrations to mark each changing season of the year. These would have been calculated using the original Lunar calendar. The Western (Julian) calendar was revised in 46BC by Julius Caesar and Augustus. It was adjusted by Pope Gregory XIII in 1582 (Gregorian) and contained a calculation error. By 1751 the error had accumulated and now amounted to 11 days. This was corrected in 1752 and in that year the third of September became the fourteenth of September.

Back to the Iron Age; the first festival was Imbolc. Held on February 1st, it was dedicated to the goddess Brigit, who was associated with pastoral matters. Imbolc was a celebration of thanks for the newborn lambs and milk beginning to flow from their ewes.

Next came Beltaine on May 1st, and was probably connected with the ancient Celtic god Belenos. Beltaine was a great cleansing fire festival with magic rituals to encourage fertile crops and cattle. The Festival of

Lughnasa on August 1st was the start of a great feast to celebrate the gathering in of the harvest and lasted for many days.

Most important and most dreaded was that of Samhain, the day of the dead, the day when the Otherworld would became visible, unleashing the supernatural forces. The greatest and most feared day in the whole calendar, Samhain was the festival of appeasement which marked the beginning of the Celtic year. It began as the mists started to rise on the eve of October 31st and continued throughout the following day, accompanied by magical divinations and superstitious ritual. The people knew that hard times lay ahead. Coldness, darkness, sickness and food shortages. Samhain heralded the arrival of winter and the long struggle for survival. Grain was rationed and cattle were slaughtered. The time had come to settle the debts of summer. Blood gifts were required as a token of their gratitude and so the terrible rituals began.

How far would these small localised groups of Celtic farm folk wander? No great distance. Life was dangerous and short and became even more difficult following the Roman invasion. Finding strength in numbers they would have become more united and more territorial, a close knit community looking out for each other in the mundane struggle to survive. Each small settlement would probably have been visited from time to time, kept informed by the representatives of an elected hierarchy of tribal leaders doing the circuit. These authority figures would be received with subservience, a mixture of fear and respect tinged, perhaps, with resentment at the intrusions. This may have been the time when they were driven to live around the margins of the peat bog - land which would have been of little use to the invaders. Within this boggy morass the sand hills and the rises of clay would have been of particular significance for both habitation and stock rearing. On the bog itself there are no signs of past human habitation. Only signs of sacrifice. From whence where they brought, these pagan victims?

Signs of a Settlement?

Motburlege was recorded in the Domesday Book in 1086. The name is a combination of the Old English words Mot+Burgh+Leah.

Mot = Meeting

Burgh = a fortified place, a stronghold, originally applied to iron age hill forts and Roman and Anglo Saxon fortifications and later to manors, manor houses, towns and boroughs.

Leah = a woodland clearing or glade and later included pastures and meadows. It is also a common local surname.

Mobberley, therefore, was originally a 'clearing at the fortification where meetings are held'.

By the same token, Burleyhurst, also on the fringes of Lindow Moss, breaks down as Burgh+Leah+Hyrst, in other words, a fortified place in a clearing on a wooded hill.

Beside Graveyard Farm in Mobberley an ancient green lane leads to a piece of land which rises quite steeply to form an extensive mound and in some places it is about 15 feet above ground level. It appears to be a sand hill. It has become a vast citadel of rabbits who - apparently since they arrived with our Norman conquerors - have tunnelled into and excavated the surrounding banks to create a massive circular warren. To the east the mound overlooks Coppock House, enclosed and sheltered by a semi circle of tall and ancient trees which play host to both tawny and long eared owls, attracted by the plentiful supply of rabbits.

The mound is in a fine defensive position. Upon reaching the highest point, it was a surprise to find such an impressive sighting point within the essentially flat terrain of Mobberley. The views were extensive; one can clearly see, to the east, Mow Cop, Bosley Cloud, Alderley Edge, the Pennine foothills and, turning to the north, Rivington Pike and the tall transmitting tower of Winter Hill. This vantage point is in the centre of the oldest and most interesting of the halls and houses which were built on the edges of the Moss - Graveyard Farm, Hollingee, Coppock House Farm, Burleyhurst Farm and Saltersley Hall. Is this the Knoll from which the little hamlet of Knolls Green took its name?. Proximity to the peat bog is only a few fields, some ten or fifteen minutes leisurely walk to the Lindow Man sacrifice site. No one has ever investigated.*
*See A Place of Sacrifice chapter.

The Medieval Period

By the Middle Ages the manorial court system and a series of charters had been introduced, forming the foundation of our legal system. These culminated in the great Magna Carta of King John in 1215. The Forest Charters, which set out the common rights of turbary, pannage and digging of marl, were incorporated in 1217 and at this time the country was marked, or meered out and boundaries were fixed, thus exerting greater controls over the agricultural tenant populations.

He that marls sand may buy land.

He that marls moss shall have no loss.

He that marls clay flings it away.

Anon. Old rhyme.

Writing in 1909 Stephan Murray provides the following description:
"The words Meere Stones and Meere Tree were used in combination, the word Meer meaning boundary. These trees and stones were sometimes placed in hedges to show where one man's portion terminated and another's began. In a

deed made in 1775, concerning an enclosure of land for the erection of the old poor house at Lindow, occurs the following phrase;

"From the Common called or known by the name of Great Lindow, as the same is now meered out by meters and bounds."

There is a field in Mobberley know as the Mere or Mere Flats. This field was formerly part of the common ploughing lands of Mobberley and was laid out in 'strips' or 'lands' appropriated to different owners or occupiers. The name may probably have been derived from the fact of the field having been 'meered out' or measured off from the common lands.

The word 'intack' in this district is not uncommonly used for a field. Newton's Intack is a field in Mobberley, not far from Lindow Common and may very likely have been a Moss Room attached to a property belonging to the Newton family, which had been enclosed."

Constables and burleymen were appointed at the manorial courts, their role being to report damage to crops and boundaries, to prevent poaching, to oversee the payment of tithes and to see that fines were levied. Mobberley Parish Council still appoint two burleymen - one of the few parishes in England still to do so.

In 1421 the manor of Wilmslow was divided between the Booths and the Traffords, but Lindow Moss was not included in the division and remained joint property of the two lords and also the freeholders.

These economic changes were socially divisive, favouring the land owners, who now controlled the peasant population. By the sixteenth century landowner power and control created rising prices. Everyone who depended on the land for their living was forced to pay whatever the owner demanded in return for the right to occupy. Those who could not afford to do so became landless labourers and wandered the countryside like the Gypsies, who had arrived into Western Europe during the fifteenth and sixteenth centuries. And, in the same way as the Gypsies, they too were now classed as itinerants - tinkers, vagabonds, rogues and thieves - and were constantly moved on by the local authorities.

History repeated itself. Just as the iron age population had been driven to the poorest lands following the Roman conquest the new landless poor were arriving to settle around the margins of the Lindow peat bog. They became known as the Bog Warriors, staking a claim to the land which no one wanted. This is how they did it:

"A short distance from Moss Lane is Paddock Hill, and across the fields is Lindow Common, where peat turf is cut for fuel. The Common is being gradually drained, cultivated and enclosed. There are some curious one-storied old cottages on the edge of the Common at different places, erected, I am informed, by the early settlers who claimed the land surrounding their dwellings as their freehold. The custom seems to have been that they were allowed as much land as they

could cultivate on condition that they could show a permanent habitation the morning following their arrival. Rough huts seem to have been put up at first and the erection of the cottages proceeded with afterwards. Several residents have told me about this custom which however is now done away with."
Stephan Murray again.

With the consent of the two land-owning families, certain portions of the Moss were enclosed in 1777 and bought under cultivation. The moss was surveyed c1850 and divide amongst landowners - both large and small - of the parish.

The field patterns are strange; long narrow strips networking the terrain. These are the Intacks and Moss Rooms, granted as rights of turbary to the forgotten marginalised folk who tried to survive on the fringes of society. The tithe maps reveal some interesting features and the original Moss Rooms are clearly marked with the names of their owners.

Nineteenth and Twentieth Centuries

Up to this point religion does not seem to have impressed itself upon the daily lives of the bog dwellers. The Tudor rages of Protestant v Catholic appear to have bypassed these lowliest of marginals. Apart from the accounts of Celtic pagan practices, which have been reasonably well documented by several Roman writers, I have failed to find any references to religious matters, other than the activities of the Quakers. It was not until the late eighteenth and early nineteenth century that the missionaries arrived, zealously determined to rescue the children of the bog dwelling savages.

The little ones were to be Sunday schooled and converted, alongside the children of the illiterate farm workers and labourers. Morris's Directory of 1874 lists James White: Profession: Local missionary. Abode: Lindow Cottage, Morley, and the Reverend Barnes-Slack appears the edition of 1880: William Slack, Vicar of Lindow, St John's Vicarage, Knutsford Road*.
* See 'Civilising the Bog Dwellers'.

The introduction of the Poor Law meant the construction of the workhouses. On the opposite side of the Altrincham Road, facing the common, they built the local Workhouse in 1773, partly funded by money left to the parish for charities. This money was lent on mortgage at $4\frac{1}{2}\%$. An act of Victorian charity towards the poor folk.

Adders were so numerous that a viper-catcher came annually to catch them. They are described as twelve to fourteen inches in length, and that their bites were poisonous and often fatal. Finney tells of a barefoot boy bitten whilst gathering cranberries. Oil was quickly applied to the bite and he was out of danger but *"He had a very cadaverous look. And all the*

lower part of his body was much swollen and puffed up, and greatly
disfigured with foul black and yellow colours as if he had been sorely
crushed and bruised."

A pointer dog, running on the Moss, was bitten on the head by an adder
and died within 12 hours.

Peat burns, and Lindow Moss can offer ordeal by fire as well as by
water. There have been some disastrous fires in dry summers. Two must
have been exceptionally bad and are recorded by Finney - 1852 and May
1865, when they burned for several weeks. Plague broke out in the area in
1866. There was another in the 1950s, which many still remember. This
one also burned for weeks, filling the air with such thick smoke that
people were forced to keep their windows closed for days on end.

Back in the 1930s - and probably for a long time before that - local
children used to play in Fir Wood, which runs from Rotherwood Road
along the eastern edge of the peat bog, and also on the bog itself. Over the
weekends and school holidays they ran wild and free, creating their own
entertainment. This frequently involved the construction of small
bonfires. One hot dry summer one of these bonfires got out of hand and
started to spread rapidly, crackling its way through the long dry grasses,
bilberry bushes and heather. Not only did the fire travel quickly
overground, it was soon creeping below the surface. Smoke rose and
belched from the cracked surface of the dried out peat. The land itself was
on fire. Panicking, the boys fled, running over the uneven surface and one
fell into a hidden ditch or trench, the remains of an old peat digging. His
dreadful screams echoed across the landscape.

They learnt their lesson the hard way. Recounted by an elderly
gentleman who was there at the time, it has never been forgotten. If these
bog fires also occurred in earlier and more superstitious times, the people
must have thought that hell itself was breaking surface.

Leycesters Firs, no longer standing but clearly marked on all the
maps, was a continuation of Fir Wood. A very dense plantation of huge
pines, presumably laid out by a member of the Leycester family, it had
remained undisturbed since first planted. Dark and mysterious, the fallen
pine needles had accumulated to a great depth so that the forest floor was
springy underfoot. This magical place was destroyed in 1941-1942, by
order of the Ministry. The timber was needed to build 'block houses',
which were similar to bunkers. These underground storage facilities were
constructed to a depth of 12 feet, the sides being shored up by the split fir
trees. Two of these block houses were built at Burleyhurst Farm to house
the radar equipment which formed part of the early warning system. The
proximity to the airfield at Ringway was obviously significant.

Men and countless cattle have drowned in the bog. As recently as the 1960s a woman who was riding her horse on the bog sank into one of the hidden pools. The fire brigade arrived with ropes and winches and struggled for many hours. When the poor horse was finally dragged free it was so exhausted its head was almost touching the ground.

Traces of the original moss and bog still remain. They are to be found, here and there, extending long soggy tentacles outwards in all directions, as if retaining custody, hanging on for dear life. Desperate, imploring or spiteful depending upon which side of the fence one is sitting. Almost a revenge attack for all those sections which have been drained and reclaimed over the centuries. But Lindow Moss does not lie curled into an obliging circle, like a sleeping cat, nor does it follow any neat rectilinear pattern to suit the developers. During the rainy seasons the reclaimed land becomes boggy and flooded. Fields and ancient paths, suddenly impossible to traverse, turn you back. There are dozens of them, an absolute maze of little routes and trackways now efficiently marked as public footpaths and rights of way by Macclesfield Borough Council. From Mobberley to Saltersley, Paddock Hill to Morley, Morley to Wilmslow. All these narrow paths leading to - nowhere! Rather like spokes radiating towards a hub which no longer exists.

CP

Lindow Moss 1900

Fletcher Moss

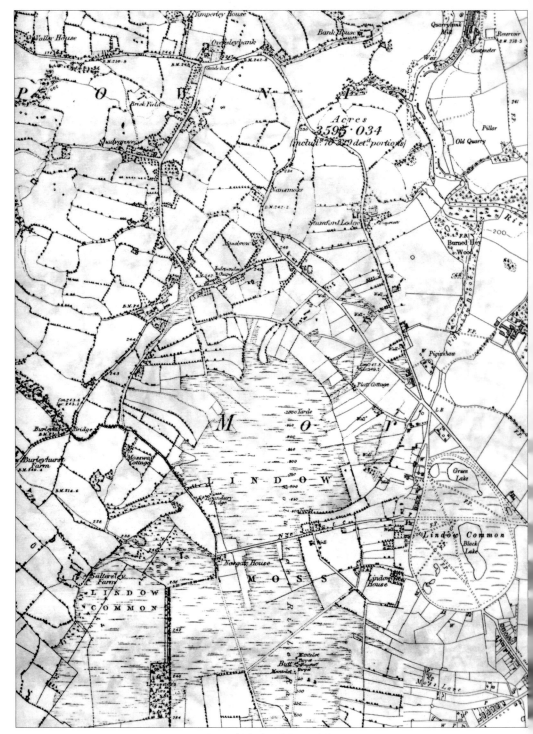

Part of Lindow Moss 1873.

Aerial view showing the peat bog within the surrounding landscape of Lindow Moss in 1990

Peat stooks drying on Saltersley Common 1900
courtesy Cheshire County Council

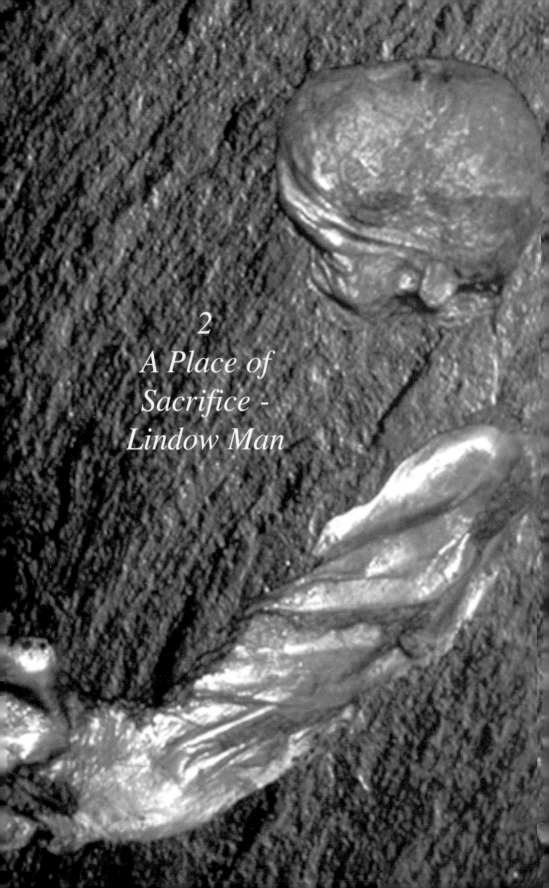

2
A Place of
Sacrifice -
Lindow Man

A Place of Sacrifice

"Who is Boggy Bo?
Him as canna rot int Burying-hole." after Stevie Davies, 'Impassioned Clay'

".... an then they dug im up agen, an when the coffin were opent there 'e were as fresh as need be, aw comfortable like, wi' is 'ed packt up wi' common Lindow black turves." Fletcher Moss 1901; Pilgrimages No. 1

Lindow Moss was a huge quaking mass of peat and water, raised up somewhat above the surrounding dry land, with definite if tentacle-like edges. It was made of vegetable remains that could not rot and so built themselves up year by year - Peat. Underneath the peat layers are ancient tree stumps that couldn't rot either, bases of pine trees that lived maybe four thousand years ago, before the Sphagnum moss choked them. They get turned up by the peat digging and can be seen lying about like bleached bones, often with identifiably piney bark still on them. Any living thing that is pushed into the peat or into a tea-coloured bog pool cannot rot either, unless it floats up to the surface. The acids and tannins, the cold and the lack of oxygen will pickle it instead.

Not surprisingly, therefore, peat diggers over the centuries working on the numerous bogs of northwest Europe have from time to time found things. Occasionally they have frightened themselves to death by coming upon human remains. It must be a horrible thing to be quietly slicing peat out of the earth for your winter fire and suddenly see a human face staring up at you, or an arm or a foot protruding from the peat, like a creature from another world. Although tanned like old leather, and gingery in hue from the peat, they are apparently perfect, every hair and and fingernail and even the fingerprints complete.

Such a find would be a local sensation, but after a while the body would be decently buried and forgotten, except perhaps in some folk memory or rhyme or tale. Sometimes however a find like this made the newspapers. Like this one:

"Our reporter on Wednesday visited Whixall, where on the previous day two men, whilst engaged in cutting out a bed of moss, disturbed some human remains. The body lay flat at full length with the face downwards. Some hair and small bits of flesh were still adhering to the skull and the ribs and legs were partly covered with flesh. It is supposed that these remains are those of a fully developed man, whose height was something like five feet eight inches. The bones were of a dark colour, and after some exposure they turned almost black."

7th September 1889 Northwich and Winsford Chronicle

Opposite: Out of the peat ...... a Bog Warrior from the iron age, 1 August 1984
courtesy Cheshire County Council

The find was a nine-day wonder, arousing much debate as to its age. The older inhabitants were questioned about any unexplained disappearances they could remember, without result. When the body began to stink it was buried in Whixall churchyard. We now think, from the description of the depth at which the body was found, that he dated perhaps from the Bronze Age.

Tollund Man

The story of Lindow man really starts in Denmark in 1950 with the discovery of Tollund man. Bog bodies had been found in Denmark before, many more than in England, and documented far back in time. But Tollund man was the first to be beautifully photographed as he lay there in his peat bed, as Lindow man was not, and the first to be permanently preserved, so that we can go to Silkeborg Museum and see him. He found a worthy biographer in Dr P.V.Glob of Aarhus University.

And, it must be said, Tollund man is beautiful in himself. Everyone has remarked on the dignity and serenity of his face, with its long nose, slightly pursed mouth and gently closed eyes. By the accident of fate, maybe, neither his face nor his comfortably curled up body were distorted by the peat. This is the image that was in everybody's mind when Lindow man turned up.

Lindow Man

Lindow Man turned up on the 1st of August 1984 - the Celtic Festival of Lughnasa! - in the processing yard at the dead end of Moor Lane. At that time peat was cut in blocks and stacked to dry on the Moss, as described in the Peat chapter. The dried blocks were trundled into the yard on a little train, then checked for bits of wood before going to the shredder. This time the conveyer was stopped in a panic when a human foot was spotted. It had been torn off below the knee and was peat-coloured and leathery. It looked so fresh that naturally the police were called. They treated the body as suspicious and connected it with a recent crime, as will be recounted below. Meanwhile however a local reporter, Rachel Pugh, perhaps knowing about Tollund Man, contacted the Cheshire archaeologist, Rick Turner. He quickly organised a painstaking search of the diggings where the current lot of peat had come. By great good fortune he spotted a flap of skin sticking out from the undug peat face. Was it the same person?

So who found Lindow Man? And where was he found? Neither question has a simple answer. Working in the yard that day were Eddy Slack and Andrew Mould. Eddy Slack was a fitter - *"but did nowt"*. Andrew Mould was a day-wager, generally *"on the Lister"* i.e. driving the little locomotive. Neither were peat diggers. Alan Mould told us:

"Uncle Les has always claimed to the family that he found the body of Lindow Man. Eddy Slack and Andy Mould 'officially' found it. Uncle Les might have been working 'black' - claiming dole."

Les Mould was working with Reg Mountford. Perhaps, however, much of the credit should go to Rick Turner.

The place in the bog where Lindow Man lay in suspended animation for so many centuries does not exist any more. Peat digging continued as soon as the furore was over. It has been dug away, and since the process was mechanised the area is just a featureless brown desert.

The police would not allow the archaeologists to take their time over digging out whoever was attached to the flap of skin. Instead, all in one day, a block of the peat bed was dug out entire, manoeuvred onto one of the little narrow gauge trucks and trundled to the yard, thence to the morgue at Macclesfield Hospital and to the laboratory excavation that revealed Lindow man to the world.

The reason for Police involvement is that an unsolved murder mystery hung over Lindow, and from the extraordinary freshness of the corpse it could have been only a recent burial.

Lindow Woman

The reason for police involvement in the Lindow man case can now be told. He wasn't the first. On Friday the 13th of May 1983 the lads on the conveyer had picked out and tossed aside a flabby deflated football from the peat. After a few days it started to stink wickedly, so they hosed it free of peat to find out what it was. It was a human head. This is one of those gruesome coincidences, because some say that football originated as a manifestation of the Celtic head cult. Something like the Ashbourne Shrovetide game played with a human head for a ball. The decayed head was identified as that of a youngish woman, and the police and many local people made the connection with an unsolved murder case.

The Reyn-Bardt Murder Case

Malika Reyn-Bardt lived in a tiny brick bungalow called Heathfield. Originally built by Mr Richardson in the 1920s to house his family, the bungalow backed onto the bog at the far end of Newgate, towards Saltersley. Malika's husband, Peter, worked at the airport for BOAC. Locally he was cruelly nicknamed 'froggy' or 'warty' because he had warts all over his forehead.

They had met in 1959. It was a whirlwind romance. Peter proposed the same day, and three days later, on the 28th March 1959, they were married. On the marriage certificate, he used his second name, Edwin, and Anglicised his surname to Rainbird. Her full name was Maria Malika di

Lifted with great difficulty from his ancient resting place within the moss, Lindow Man is transferred to a makeshift bier ....

courtesy Cheshire County Council

.... and stretchered towards his next destination - the hospital mortuary at Macclesfield

courtesy Cheshire County Council

Heathfield, originally built by Mr Richardson, later belonged to the Reyn-Bardts and became the scene of the murder of Malika, to which Peter Reyn-Bardt confessed many years later.

Fernandez. It was hardly a marriage made in heaven. He was a known homosexual; she was a Spanish prostitute.

Sometime in 1960 Malika disappeared.

In 1982 Peter Reyn-Bardt was doing time in jail for something else. He boasted to his cell mates of having done away with his wife. He said that he had killed her in their little dining room, then chopped her up, tried to burn her and finally buried her in the bog (the Celtic threefold death!). A report came to the police in Knutsford, under Detective Sergeant George Abbott, who cross-examined him. Reyn-Bardt denied everything. They diligently dug over the garden and the bog behind it, but *'found nowt'*. Stalemate. The case had to be dropped.

Then the head on the conveyer turned up. Pathologists' reports stated that it was that of a woman aged between 30 and 50 and was approximately 20-50 years old. The police decided to confront him with the skull, and then to take him back to the supposed scene of the crime. At first he stuck to his denial, but when taken back to the cottage he went to pieces, confessed, and showed the police where he had buried her. But there was nothing there.

Meanwhile the head, which had been living under the Detective Sergeant's bed, was sent off for a confirmatory Carbon-14 dating. Was it pre- or post- 1960? The result came back before the trial. The Lab Chief said dryly "I think they were very surprised". That was an understatement. The female head was dated to AD 410, or given a margin of error between AD 210 and AD 610. An ancient woman. Nevertheless the trial proceeded. Peter Reyn-Bardt was convicted of murder at Chester Crown Court and and sentenced to Life imprisonment.

It is a unique case, because once the only piece of evidence was proven to be inadmissible - Lindow woman is not only 1600 years old but is not now thought to be a woman at all, but a man, the conviction rested purely on his confession.

Peter Reyn-Bardt is now released from prison. Malika Reyn-Bardt may still be lying in the bog somewhere. Or she may be alive in Spain. There is only his confession to say that she was murdered at all, or is even dead.

Lindow III

A human head in a bog is big news, especially when connected with a murder case. A whole bog man - well, half a one, - especially one who has been gruesomely put to death, is a worldwide sensation. A third body is too much, not newsworthy, especially when it consist only of shredded bits. This one turned up in 1987, on the conveyer as usual. This time the archaeologists were there from the start, unhampered by the police, and were able to carry out controlled digs. In the end however Lindow III adds little to the story. It is quite likely in fact that Lindow I, the head found in 1983, and Lindow III, the shredded body found four years later, are one and the same person. Probably a man.

DNA testing would prove this theory one way or another. Once again science can tell us less than we expect, because unfortunately DNA is entirely destroyed by bog acids.

****

Lindow Man Re-examined

The one and only incontrovertible fact about Lindow Man is the man himself. Half of him at any rate. There he lies on his bed of peat in a dark corner of the British Museum, half raised up on his left elbow, but with his face squashed and creased as though the weight of the centuries was an intolerable burden, as indeed it must be.

Poor man. He is displayed simply as another object in a vast collection, with no context, no human dignity, of no more or less significance than a bronze shield or a corroded iron sword. Visitors crane over his darkened bed uncomprehendingly, discuss who or what he is in one of the languages of the world, miss the brief noncommittal explanatory card on the wall, and pass on. He is just a thing.

And yet he is a man, astonishingly well preserved after all his ordeals. Better preserved in many respects than the much more glamourous Egyptian mummies who are desiccated, their guts and brains removed. His gingery hair and beard, stained by the bog, have darkened and his leathery skin is looking dry and whitish in places. He has been turned over: in the bog he was face down. Only his top half is there, cut off three inches below his belly button, apart from the detached foot that was found in the yard. He has no left hand, and his lower left arm and right arm and hand are reduced to bone - but there are still nails on a couple of his fingers. Whole speculative biographies have been written on the basis of those nails. His face is squashed up not just from top to bottom but diagonally, giving him a grotesquely rueful expression. He has had a nasty bash on the top of his head - two actually, if you look closely, and another at the base of his skull.

He took nothing with him. No clothes, no bag, no tools or weapons, no money. No name. Nothing but a scrap of something round his upper left arm, and a very thin knotted cord round his neck. The arm band is identified as fox fur (more whole biographies) and the cord as a garotte (not just biographies but a sensational and gruesome death).

Before we leave him in the BM it is worth looking at a couple of other things that may shed some light on this mysterious man. In the same room is a magnificent display of Celtic torcs, which are heavy neck ornaments nearly always of gold. Like a gangster's Mercedes in Kiev or Moscow today, a torc was visible - and most importantly, mobile - wealth and status.

Torcs are twisted. They show visible torque. Twisting, throttling. An odd image for personal adornment. It is reminiscent of Lindow Man's garotte.

One final thought: most things in this world change and decay. What lasts? Not much. Gold does, immortal gold, which is why it is so prized. So does a body pushed into a peat bog.

The other thing, co-incidentally displayed close by, is not thing at all but another poor naked man to be gaped at. GINGER is another star. He is not British but Egyptian and three and a half thousand years older, and was preserved by hot dry sand not cold wet peat. Like Lindow Man, he has character but no identity. The name Ginger is the nickname that seems to be necessary to us. We have no idea who he was really.

'GINGER'
courtesy Louise Sutherland

When we come to re-examine Lindow Man it is surprising to realise how little science can tell us. It can tell us the minutiae of his gut contents but not the really important things. We have so few clues. Except the scrap of fox fur round his upper left arm, and a piece of thin cord knotted round his neck, no artifacts of any significance have ever been found in the bog either, which would help to answer some of the many questions.

What Did He Look Like?

We know what Lindow Man looks like. We can go and see him any time in the British Museum. We can see the remains of his hair and beard, his creased forehead and folded over ear, and his poor squashed face.

Manchester Medical School, under Richard Neave, specialises in the reconstruction of faces and heads from skulls, achieving some startling results. This was an unusual case, because the skin and flesh were still present. Nevertheless the team took his head down to the skull by means of X-rays, straightened it out until it looked right, made a model of it and then built up a new face on top of it using their established techniques.

Until it looked right. Facial reconstruction is put forward as a scientific process, but at critical moments it is more of an imaginative art. The reconstructed head of Lindow man may be accurate, or it may not.

Apart from the scrap of fur round his upper arm Lindow Man is naked. One or two of the bog bodies that have been found have items of clothing, such as Tollund Man's hat, but mostly they went to their watery graves with nothing, not even clothes. New evidence suggests that Lindow Man may have been painted. Evidence for body painting is especially interesting because the materials are near at hand and can still be picked up. At Alderley Edge, such a dominant landscape feature at Lindow, bright blue, green, yellowish and red stones can all be found, around Engine Vein for example. Two thousand years ago these must have been much more plentiful. The stones are soft and sometimes muddy and it would not have been difficult to make paint out of them. We think of the ancient Britons as fearsomely painted blue with woad, but here a multicoloured effect with mineral pigments seems more likely.

When Was He Alive?

This is a vexed question. Again we expect science to give an answer, but Science is equivocal. Anything that has been alive can be dated by the rate of decay of Carbon 14. The peat surrounding Lindow Man has been dated to 350 - 500 BC. The pollen record confirms this, so it is a secure date range.

Lindow Man himself has been dated by Oxford to 1940 years old, plus or minus 25 years. That makes his lifetime in the first century after the birth of Christ, say AD 30-60. Harwell Laboratory disagreed. They came out with an age of 1575 years plus or minus 70, so according to them he lived four centuries later, in say AD 400-30.

The two dates are widely different, with no overlap. In Oxford's estimation he was a Celt living in a pre-Roman Britain, but according to Harwell he lived in a well-established Roman colony. Both estimated dates disagree with that of the peat in which he lay, which was at least half a millennium older still.

How can this be explained? Some would say that the police were right all along. Lindow Man is not ancient at all, but a relatively recent murder victim whose body in its pickling has taken on the apparent date of the bog. If this is discounted, and it does not answer the discrepancy between the peat and the body, we are still left with a problem.

Secure dating can usually be achieved by correlating the C14 date with circumstantial evidence - pottery say, or clothes. Ginger for instance, in the British Museum, was buried with pots and other bits and pieces characteristic in their style of his period. Lindow Man had nothing, and nothing significant has ever been found in or near the bog - which is odd in itself. So all we have are the three widely differing dates.

Velson Horie, who was the museum conservator at the 1984 dig, thinks that they cut a hole in the peat and pushed him underneath, into the watery layer below the growing peat surface. This means that he came to lie in peat that was already four or five hundred years old. The embarrassing discrepancy between the two dates for Lindow Man can be due to different calculations and pre treatments to compensate for the leaching in of Carbon from the peat.

The fact is that we do not have a secure date for the lifetime of Lindow Man, any more than we know his name. For the purpose of argument I am assuming what most archaeologists have assumed, that he was a Celt and that he was alive either when the Romans were in control of the area or immediately before, when they were on their way. A hoard of low-denomination Roman money was found in 1995 on Alderley Edge. The coins gave a date of about 300 AD. Beneath it a square shaft corkscrewing down into the Edge was excavated. At the bottom of it there was a piece of wood, the 'manky plank', which gave a date of 75AD. This seems very early for Romans to be mining in Cheshire. A fascinating link with those ancient miners was the discovery amongst the rubbish infilling the shaft of some chunks of top quality lead ore. Why was it not used? The most likely explanation is that it was thrown back, when the shaft was exhausted, as a thank offering to the earth or to the Gods of the earth for what it had provided, and perhaps to encourage them to make some more. Who knows? It is the sort of thing the Pagan Celts would have done, or the Romans, or indeed any miner today without thinking too much about it.

Shall we guess that Lindow Man was alive when that shaft was being dug?

Who Was He?

Not a single one of the bog bodies found on Britain or Scandinavia has a name, or any inkling of an identity. They have a lot of personality, but we don't know who they are. Tollund Man especially is so beautiful and so perfect that we feel that we know him. But we don't. We have no idea who he is.

Names last longer than almost everything. We remember the

famous names of history centuries after their mortal remains and deeds are gone. When a person dies their name is recorded, on a death certificate, on a tombstone, on a Mummy case. The funeral effigies in a church, or the Egyptian Mummies in a museum only take on a real meaning when we know who they are. There is a need for us to give people like Tollund Man or Lindow Man a name, because they are so palpably present with us. Ginger for instance, who lies in the British Museum and is almost as well-known an ancient Egyptian as Tutankhamen, IS Ginger, despite the fact that we have not the faintest idea who he really is. Lindow Man was dubbed in all the newspapers of the time Pete Marsh, or Lindow Pete. Anne Ross calls him Lovernius, naming him by his fox fur band, and identifying him by a chain of very dodgy reasoning as a Irish Druid Prince.

If Lindow Man and his bog brothers and sisters were important, it seems odd that no name or the faintest echo of a name has survived. Maybe, when they were stripped of their clothes, they were stripped of their identity as well.

I am resisting giving him a name. We think, because of his mode of death, that he was a Celt. We see no reason to think he was anything other than a local man. The next task is to look for his home.

Where Did He Live?

Today there are habitation sites around the bog including some that are ancient, and there are more ephemeral settlements on the bog or on the sand islands. In the Iron Age the bog would probably have been uninhabitable, a huge living entity itself, slowly growing and rising, infested with mosquitoes and adders, and very dangerous to unwary feet. It did however provide a perfect defence, so dry sites at the edge would have been favoured places.

So where were the settlements? It is quite possible that some of the habitations of today represent places where people lived as long ago as Lindow Man. Saltersley on its sand peninsula, at the nexus of straight trackways, is a good candidate. The sand hill sheltering Saltersley was apparently anciently called Crown Knoll, or Knowle. Hollingee is another, with its hollow road leading straight to the bog.

What about places which are settlements no longer? We have identified at least two possible sites, uninhabited today but dry, defensible and linked by trackways. The best one, spotted by Jeremy Milln, is immediately northwest of Graveyard farm. It is by the trackway from Knolls Green to Saltersley, which could have been a long distance route from the salt wyches either into Wilmslow via Newgate or northwards to Styal and Manchester. It is a fine breezy hill of seven acres, called simply

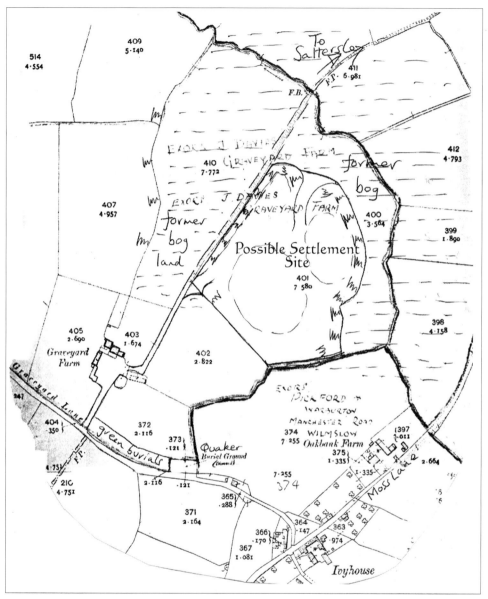

Map showing the area surrounding Graveyard Farm and field 401, the possible iron age settlement site.

Field 401, sandy and surrounded by a steep bank, provides extensive views in all directions. Tentacles of the bog probably once encircled it. Remnants of a roadway curve up onto the hilltop from the brook crossing. Another old track connects with Graveyard Farm.

This mound, sheltered by ancient hedges, stands alongside Coppock House, on the opposite side of the brook to Field 401. It is surprisingly close to the edge of the peat bog.

Field 401, sandy, with a steep bank all the way round especially on the curving north and east sides. Tentacles of the bog probably once encircled it. There appears to be a roadway curving up onto the hilltop from the brook crossing, and another leading towards Graveyard Farm. Today the site is empty of human habitation, but it is a veritable Rabbit City. They love the steep sandy banks that edge it.

Another possible settlement site is Paddock Hill, again identified by Jeremy but this time from the map rather than by eye. It is a twin to Field 401, a little bigger - say nine acres - and just a few fields away to the south and west. The name Paddock Hill is clear enough, but where is the hill? If you visit the well known Plough and Flail there does not appear to be a hill, but if you walk over the curving path next to it you are brought to a stop by a sudden scarp downwards, overlooking a big sunken area - dug-out peat bog - towards Moss Lane to the northwest. The hill is convincing enough when you are on it, with wide views all round, but the soil appears to be more clayey than sandy - the rabbits don't like it - and altogether it is not quite such a favourable spot as Field 401.

This summer, 2002, a mysterious Iron Age Bog Town is being excavated by teams from Exeter and Hull Universities. It is over in Yorkshire, a few miles north of Doncaster on the A19, at a place called Askern, Today there is not much sign of a bog, indeed it appears to be rather arid corn-growing country. In the Iron Age it was an enormous bog forming a sort of inland delta of the River Humber. The Askern site is on its edge. It consists of two slightly raised islands of sand linked by a causeway, each one with two ditches and a bank around it. Actually it is much less impressive than our putative Graveyard site.

There is little to see at first. Just flat rectangular areas of sand laid bare by the stripping off of the topsoil, each one with a squatting student scratching away with an archaeologist's trowel in the hot sun. However, look a bit harder and dark discolourations of the sand can be seen, Look harder still and they fall into a pattern. Roundish grey blotches in a line, regularly spaced, round the edge; that must be a stockade of some sort, the wood rotted away to leave the dark stain. Bigger stains in a circle, with a couple in the middle as well; that must be a building, with two big central posts and a ring of smaller ones for the perimeter. Occasionally a stump has survived in the ground, together with a few bits of stone that were used to jam it in tight.

The mysterious thing about the site is that so little else has been found. No pots for instance. Pots are the prime tool of archaeology. No bones, no metal. Virtually nothing. Either the Askern people had nothing, or they were preternaturally tidy.

There are interesting parallels here with Lindow. The settlement at the very edge of the bog is just what we have been looking for at Lindow, and may possibly have found. The lack of material remains is the same. It seems likely that these cultures were one of the few that have existed without baked clay pots. They probably cooked directly on the fire, or heated stones in a fire and then threw them into water in a non-durable container of some kind, perhaps of wood. There are written accounts of people living in the Scottish or Irish bogs as late as the eighteenth century who had virtually nothing, indeed some of those same people were in Manchester in the early nineteenth century still with virtually nothing.

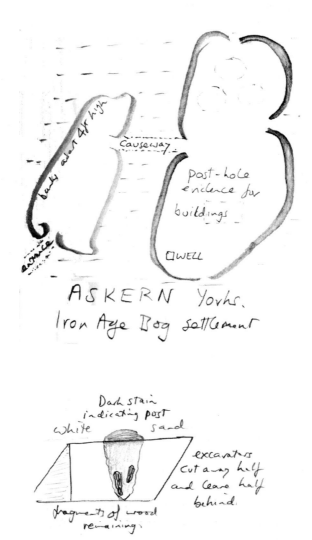

How Did He Die?

The title of the April 1998 Horizon TV programme about Lindow Man was OVERKILL. Which sums it up. Lindow Man died of multiple causes, in such a way as to rule out accident or battle or highway robbery. His death brings to mind such horribly complicated deaths as Hanging, Drawing and Quartering, or Violent Humiliation, Flogging and Crucifixion.

The forensic experts found that he had been bashed on the head, twice, and again possibly at the back of the neck. He had been strangled with a thin garotte. He had been stabbed with a thin knife in the neck. And he had been pushed in to a pool in a peat bog. All this can still be seen with careful observation at the British Museum, although the knife was never found.

That's four lethalities. The explanation that has found most favour is that the poor man was a sacrifice, the ultimate sacrifice, to the bloodthirsty Celtic Gods. Perhaps in a time of desperate hardship or looming defeat - the Romans were coming. The Celtic method was a threefold death, not a fourfold one. Celts liked to do things in threes, just as we often do today - a beginning, a middle and an end. It is not difficult to rationalise Lindow man's death into a threefold execution, but we have to be aware that we are making the facts fit the explanation.

Lindow Man, a well set-up fellow in good health, strong and stocky, was led willingly or resignedly to the sacrifice site. We can only guess where that was and only imagine the scene. He was hit from behind, hard enough to break his teeth. Then he was strangled, and while the cord was tightened a cut was made into his neck to release a dramatically copious fountain of blood. Perhaps it was collected into a ceremonial cauldron, as has been found at Gundestrup in Denmark. Finally, perhaps even now not clinically dead, he was sent through the still reflecting pool in the peat bog into the nether world. What for?

Why Did He Die?

We don't know is the straight answer. But that does not stop us from speculating.

Tollund Man, despite his calm expression, was strangled, then shoved in the bog. The noose is still round his neck. P.V. Glob's book makes the case that he and his fellows were the victims of ritual human sacrifice.

The unnecessarily complicated death of Lindow Man suggests a ritual too, and most, but not all, archaeologists interpret Lindow man's death as a sacrifice. Further evidence comes from the fragments of burnt bread in his stomach, which has been interpreted as a selection ritual, where the chosen victim is the one who picks the burnt piece of a shared cake. Those of us who burn the breakfast toast may be sceptical of this. The other exciting thing recovered by analysis of his stomach contents was some Mistletoe pollen. Four grains to be precise. Mistletoe was central to the the rituals of that mythical priesthood, the Druids.

Archaeologists sometimes admit, laughing at themselves a little, that the word Ritual means We Don't Understand It.

Most authors are anxious to stress the difference between us and them, making nervous caveats like *"care must be taken not to impose our twenty-first century values and ethics on ancient societies"*
This is true, but it is also true that our Iron Age ancestors were essentially the same as us. Our society has changed but we have not. It is interesting therefore to consider, not how different we are from Lindow Man but how similar are we? And to examine ourselves and see if we can understand what made them kill him.

In 2002 we still make offerings or sacrifices, in trivial and unthinking ways. How many time capsules were buried to mark the Millennium? The turning of the year and the passing of the seasons is still important to us. We mark midwinter by the biggest blowout of them all, a two-week shut down for Christmas and New Year.

The most important Celtic festival was Samhain, marking the end of one year and the beginning of the next. It was on the first day of November, its eve was on the last of October. The church took over Samhain as All Saints and All Souls days, a time to remember the dead and in some countries to go and have a party at your ancestor's graveside. All Saints eve, Hallowe'en, the eve of Samhain, certainly has not lost its grip on us. Beltaine or May Day was the other great festival, a more joyful one associated with the lighting of great fires over which or between which you had to pass for purification and protection. In some countries it has transferred itself to midsummer, as in Ukraine, where Ivana Kupala is on St John's Eve, midsummer, with great bonfires and fiery wheels of plaited grass.

Do we ever try to intercede with God to make the year turn and the seasons pass? Not at Harvest Festival. That is a thanksgiving. All good things around us are sent from heaven above. An older festival though, still held in many places in the spring, is called Rogation. It is an asking not a thanksgiving service, when God is asked to send us good things, with the symbolic planting and blessing of seeds.

The ancient Gods were unlikely to provide anything good or even make the seasons turn and summer come round again, unless they were asked. It was seen as a bargain, something had to be offered in return.

Do we sometimes look for a scapegoat, enjoying the spectacle of somebody, especially somebody who 'had it coming', humiliated and brought low? It is an English characteristic. Remember the downfall of Neil Hamilton MP, in 1997.

Do we enjoy violence? We may like to think that we do not, but violence is part of our make-up, and surrogate violence is the stuff of entertainment. Do we get excited by communal violence? Mix with a football crowd or a political demonstration to find out.

Why Was He Buried In A Bog?

There was no Celtic heaven. Watery places were the gateway to the other world for the Celts. Lindow Man was killed in the prime of life, and was sent to the other world via a fearsome watery place. He was not buried in good ground where his body could rot in peace. Instead he was pushed down into a place that prevents decay, where he could not rot. The Iron Age Celts must have known this as well as we do. Carbon 14 dating has shown that Lindow Man drifted up in the mushy peat, slowly rising underneath the top layer. It is possible that the Celts knew this too, that his body would slowly drift upwards. In 1984 he appeared again, prematurely and unceremoniously as it happens in the course of peat digging. It is possible that the Celts hoped for this too. In other words, that he was ritually killed and pushed into the bog for future reference.

A couple of miles from Lindow looms the equally mysterious Alderley Edge. On top of the Edge on the main road is The Wizard Inn. In the legend the Wizard stopped a farmer from Mobberley - always from Mobberley - who was on his way to Macclesfield to sell a fine horse. The farmer refused to sell to the Wizard, but although all admired his horse nobody would buy, and on the way home when the Wizard re-appeared he agreed to sell. The Wizard led him, by a complicated route that again is always the same in all tellings, to a place under the ground where a King slept, with his knights and their steeds, but just wanting one more white horse, ready to wake and rise in a time of direst need.

A King Under the Ground. Ready to wake and rise again in time of direst need. Do we have an echo here? Legends almost always have a kernel of truth in them. The Alderley legend with its list of places probably enshrines a vital boundary or frontier. The King under the ground could be an echo of Lindow man or somebody like him, hidden but preserved under the ground ready to rise again in time of need.
And one final question:-

How Come He Ended Up In The BM?

Lindow man was at Manchester Museum, on temporary exhibition, twice, in 1987 and 1990. There he was the centrepiece, fully interpreted, given a

What brought him to this?
Something which we were never intended to see, a life abruptly terminated. Lindow Man was born into a hard, superstitious and unforgiving world. The head is distorted by the weight of the peat which preserved him for centuries within the moss. The sinew garotte around his throat is clearly visible.

courtesy Cheshire County Council

Part of the atmospheric Lindow Man exhibition at Manchester Museum, where he was on display surrounded by a large collection of iron age artefacts and votive offerings.

courtesy Manchester Museum

context and surrounded by a Lindow-in-the-Iron-Age ambience, as far as a museum in Manchester can do so. The exhibitions were hugely successful. On each occasion the question on everyone's lips was, Why can he not stay here? Why should he be in London? This is a question that dogs every museum, and it is a valid one.

The hastily-assembled team who carried out the disinterment of Lindow Man from the bog and his subsequent examination included representatives from both the Manchester Museum and the British Museum, as well as from the Cheshire Archaeological service. We are told that there was some argument over his long term resting place, even over the poor man's corpse, like unseemly relatives quarrelling over the will before the dead person is even buried.

The BM won. He was considered to be of National importance and therefore the National museum had the prior claim. In fact it was a fait accompli, because the BM, knowing how these things are done, had gone straight to the owner of the site. Who was, surprisingly, Heinz. Yes, the baked beans people; see the Peat chapter.

In the BM he is seen by many more people, from all over the world, but he has lost his connection with Cheshire. More people see him, but fewer people know who or what he is or derive any meaning from him. He is, as has been said already, just another disassociated object in a vast and wondrous worldwide collection.

Are There More Out There?
Several bodies were found all at once. None before, none since. It was the same at Whixall. This would suggest no. Nevertheless the modern peat digger must eye each scoopful of peat as it is lifted up from the bog with apprehension. Lindow man and the others haunt the site. Were there only so few, or was it an annual sacrifice? MH

Rogation service at Sutton, Macclesfield 2002. Beating the Bounds always took place at Rogationtide

courtesy Alice Hyde

3
Trackways
Across the Bog

Trackways Across The Bog

"We can't get down, and if we did get down, we'd find all that green land a nasty bog I'll warrant. Phew! can you smell it?"

Sam in The Two Towers - Lord of the Rings

There are no roads over Lindow. You have to drive round it. The roads all skirt round the edge of the bog. The road from Wilmslow to Mobberley and Knutsford swings south to avoid it, and the Wilmslow to Altrincham Road swings considerably north. Burleyhurst Lane makes its gingerly way along the north west fringes of the bog from Morley to Knolls Green, and Racecourse Road in Wilmslow runs round the sand hill of Lindow Common. This was not even a road until the 1890s, but a Gypsy racetrack, as is recounted elsewhere.

Making a proper road across the bog would be a difficult operation. The Liverpool and Manchester Railway, which when it opened in 1830 was the first serious railway in the world, had to cross Chat Moss which is even bigger than Lindow and only a few miles north. The toll bridge over the Mersey at Warburton leads to it. On the first day of construction the engineer appointed by Stephenson slipped off the line of planks laid over the bog and began to sink. The more he struggled the deeper he sank and it took the efforts of several workmen to drag him to safety. He was said to be 'much disheartened'. Stephenson's plan was to float the line over the bog, spreading the load with a mat of heather and branches piled layer upon layer. Sometimes it seemed that they could be throwing branches and brushwood in for ever only to see them swallowed up by the mire. But in the end it worked. The track over Chat Moss has proved to be exceptionally good, with a natural springiness. A modern locomotive, many times heavier than the old 'Rocket' travelling at speed over the floating line is a sight to see. A wave of compression travels with the train through the bog and the whole ground rises and falls for several yards around, like waves on the surface of the water.

Until the mid 1990s the peat diggers here at Lindow, as at Dane's Moss near Macclesfield and Whixall Moss near Wem, used a little two-foot gauge railway system to transport peat to the depot. The rough sleepers spread the load sufficiently over the bog, although sometimes the track did sink unevenly and the little loco was tipped sideways into the mire. Then it was just a matter of crow-barring it back on again, with much cursing no doubt. The present-day peat diggers at Lindow use the Stephenson method for their tractor ways, piling branches and wood chips

Opposite: The old Roman Road near Middlewich, part of the ancient Cheshire salt route which runs to Manchester via Saltersley.

Remnants of old rail track revealed by current peat extraction on Lindow Moss.

Train carrying peat across Lindow peat bog
Sydney Wheeler collection, courtesy Wilmslow Historical Society

to spread the load.

There may be no roads over Lindow, but there are plenty of green trackways. They are a particular feature of Lindow, very distinctive and rather beautiful. Always straight, raised above the level of the surrounding land, with deep ditches of peaty water on either side, and lined with silver birch trees to make a green tunnel. They are much used by dog walkers and riders. But not fit for motors! Cyril Wood, of Newgate, remembers trying to drive along one of the bog tracks:

"I drove a taxi for a while when I was about 16 or 17. Took Lizzie Munnerley home once - she was flaked out in the back. Been drinking with the RAF fellows. I dropped her off at her track*, then I thought I'd go and visit a girlfriend on Moor Lane - take the shortcut along Rotherwood. Well I got the taxi stuck on Battery Lane. I walked back and knocked on the door of that cottage on the corner of Newgate. Loads of hillbillies poured out and pushed it back up to Newgate."

*See Lizzie chapter

Nowadays these paths are reasonably firm and dry. Only a springiness in the ground tells of the deep peat layers underfoot. Once they must have been treacherous indeed, probably just a line of planks or brushwood. A step off the straight and narrow way, as Stephenson's engineer found, could be fatal. Even today a horse or a cow falling into one of the ditches takes many hours to drag out and can be so exhausted by its ordeal that it may not survive. Bruce Mould remembers such an occasion, spending a whole day rescuing a cow from a ditch. He lost a day's pay, and the farmer did not give him anything either, which still rankles.

Today Lindow Moss is almost tamed, the peat drained and dug away. Once upon a time the whole of Lindow was raised above the surrounding land, a huge peaty morass, growing, featureless, and as soft as porridge. How could the paths be made across such a quagmire? How could you know you were on the path, and not wandering off into the slough of despond, especially in the mists which must have haunted it?

Sometimes it is possible to cross such a dangerous place by intricate knowledge of it, by knowing exactly where the firmer bits are and the dryer refuges. A path like this will dodge about secretively. Gollum took Frodo and Sam over such a path.

"The hobbits soon found that what looked like one vast fen was really an endless network of pools, and soft mires, and half strangled water courses. Among these a cunning eye and foot could thread a wandering course."

Tolkien describes the Passage of the Marshes vividly:

"They went slowly in single file: Gollum, Sam, Frodo ..... It was dreary

and wearisome. Cold clammy water still held sway in this forsaken country. The only green was the scum of livid weed on the dark greasy surfaces of the sullen waters. Dead grasses and rotting weeds loomed up in the mists like ragged shadows of long forgotten summers."

The Lord of the Rings, Book 4

The other way is to strike out boldly, aim for a distant point, and MAKE a path. It can be done by laying down boards or logs or brushwood into the mire to stop yourself sinking. One such has been found in the Somerset Levels, a Bronze Age track named the Sweet Track after the person who discovered it. It was made by laying a line of logs, then driving stakes in to make an X shape held by the logs, and finally laying planks in the upper part of the X, clear of the bog surface. An archaeological reconstruction has been tried out, and it works but is pretty treacherous because the planks are liable to tip sideways.

Because all the Lindow trackways are so straight they are not the kind Gollum found. They must have been MADE across the bog, like the Sweet Track. Lindow was probably too deep to use stakes, so we can imagine a narrow line of brushwood and branches, which would have slowly sank but still provided sufficient firmness to walk on, provided you didn't wander off. Crossing Lindow safely to reach dry land on the other side must have been akin to bringing a boat in to harbour by using navigation marks lined up to show the one safe approach. I can imagine lining up a point on a distant hill with a mark on the far side of the bog, a big tree perhaps, or a stone, and then stepping out across the quivering morass reasonably confident that, so long as the two marks are in line, I am not going to wander off the straight and narrow and drown.

"Why did you not look for the steps?"

"Fear followed me so hard that I fled the next way, and fell in."

"there are good and substantial steps, placed even through the very midst of the Slough, but at such a time as this such steps are hardly seen; or if they be, men through the dizziness of their heads step beside, and then they are bemired to purpose, notwithstanding the steps be there."

Pilgrim's Progress

What were the landmarks that the trackways were aligned on?

Alderley Edge is the prime feature. Remembering that it was bare of trees until the Stanley plantings of the eighteenth century, any feature on its skyline would have been a perfect beacon. And of course there is the Beacon, a pimple of rock and earth almost certainly an ancient tumulus, on which stood in later times a little stone tower which is still there as scattered stones. The National Trust would like to rebuild it. Nowadays the Beacon is deeply embosomed in trees, and useless as a landmark - in fact it is quite hard to find. When the Edge was bare it would have been as visible from afar as Lyme Cage, which is a clear sighting to the northeast, or White Nancy above Bollington to the east.

No alignment on the Alderley Edge Beacon will work today because it is hidden in the trees, so it can only be done with a map. The best alignment appears to be the green trackway, dead straight, from near Mrs Eckert's farm, The Yews*, to Upcast Lane at Davenport Green. From The Yews it probably diverged slightly to Barlow Farm and Coppock House, but the southern section is lined up perfectly on the Beacon.
*See 'Row of Trees' section.

It is interesting that nearly all the natural high points in the locality are made more effective by a man-made structure on top, serving not only to emphasise it but also to give an exact point to aim at. Lyme Cage and White Nancy, Mow Cop with its mock castle, The fat tower of Wincle Mast on Wincle Minn, Winter Hill with its tall slender mast plus little followers, Mottram Church. The present structures are not very old, but they are likely to have been built where earlier markers were, as we know was the case with Lyme Cage. The Bowstones are an ancient example, right at the top of Lyme Park. They would have been a fine landmark on the long slope leading up to the ridge from the west before the white farmhouse (why white?) was built on the very top.

A landmark does not have to be a structure or even an eminence. It can be a notch. Bosley Cloud by Congleton is not crowned with a distinguishing structure, although there were several significant rock outcrops prior to the building of the railway, the Sugar Rock, the Raven Rock and most significant of all, the Bully Thrumble, a giant stone corkscrew that rose 60 feet into the sky. All were blown up, an astonishing act of vandalism, and used as hardcore for the railway bed. The base of the Bully Thrumble is still visible amongst the undergrowth and the strange Cat Stone survives. We can always recognise it though, from any distance, because it has a huge bite out of it. The bite is a quarry and probably not ancient, but it shows that a cutting-away is as good a landmark as a building-up.

A long V-shaped notch or groove, like a hollow road on the slope of a hill, is an especially effective guide when climbing out of the valley below, because it can be kept visually in line, like a rifle sight. There appears to be a perfect example at Hollingee. Overgrown today, it is a hollow road leading from the farm straight through a sand hill and onto the bog. It seems to serve no purpose - there is no route across the bog here today - but curiously enough the other end of it is still there; the furthest end of Moor Lane leading to Horticon. If this is correct, then once upon a time there was a direct route from Hollingee - clearly an ancient place with its moat - to the bog settlement at Stormy Point and then on

Moat at Hollingee

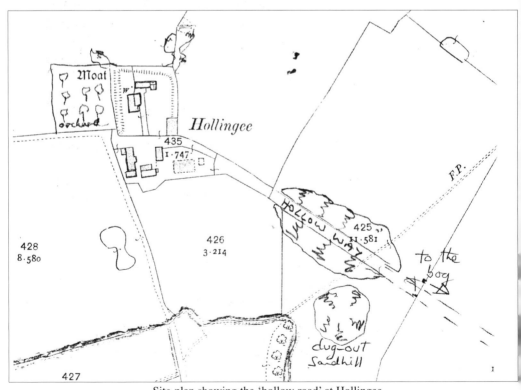

Site plan showing the 'hollow road' at Hollingee

towards Alderley Edge. In fact, the landmark in the opposite direction appears to be the Alderley Edge beacon again.

Is Saltersley itself a landmark? When Newgate was made - its name suggests that it was new once - it diverged from the Altrincham Road at the Wilmslow corner of Lindow Common. Leading straight across the common, where it is just a footpath today, it crosses the Racecourse and then, changing its angle a little, strikes off straight as an arrow across the bog to the sand hill of Saltersley. Here it is diverted because there is now a lake in the way. The sand hill - it was called Crown Knoll - was dug out by Ralph Croxall in the 1950s, and the flooded sandpit is a popular fishing venue. There may have been something on the knoll that guided travellers, or the something may have been the stone box of Saltersley itself. In the other direction the landmark was probably the lone erratic boulder, though it seems much too small today, at the north end of the Black Lake on Lindow Common where all the paths cross. That stone lines up with Lyme Cage in the distance.

Long distance trackways in Cheshire are especially associated with the vital trade in SALT. Salt was the only way to preserve meat and fish over the long winter. There are well-known salt ways radiating out from the salt towns of Cheshire. They are often marked by their names, such as The Salt Box, a little house on the Old Buxton Road in Macclesfield. And Saltersley of course. White and Wych are also salt names. Whitegate presumably means salt road, nothing to do with white paint or gates. The famous book 'The Old Straight Track' by Alfred Watkins, written as long ago as 1925, though it was a favourite of the 1960s New Age movement. Watkins writes:- *"In noting place-names on the straight track it gradually becomes evident that the local characteristics of the spot are often a minor influence; the track itself, the men who made it, who came along it, or the goods they carried giving names to the places all along the line."*

Poring over maps with a ruler may be a sign of incipient madness, but Saltersley is on a direct straight route from Middlewich, where the Romans developed a major salt industry from earlier works, to the crucial Mersey crossing at Stockport. The route is marked by the A50 between the sharp bends at Allostock and Radbroke Hall, and then by Knolls Green, Mobberley, where the Bird in Hand pub stands at the south end of the bog, which several people have told us was the site of a Roman road. The trackway across the bog goes past Graveyard Farm and the possible Iron Age settlement Field 401* to reach Saltersley, which was probably a staging post. Northwards the route was to Morley Green and on to the equally crucial Bollin crossing at the north end of Styal Mill where the packhorse bridge still stands.

*See 'A Place of Sacrifice' chapter.

A second route could have gone via Newgate and Wilmslow to Adlington, then on into the hills by Saltersford and White Hall and over into Derbyshire - but perhaps we are getting carried away.

Howard Hodson adds substance to the supposition of an important trade route via Saltersley in his 'The Story of Wilmslow' 1971 (p36):

"The transport of materials and finished goods was no doubt by packhorse. There is a strong tradition, readily accepted by local historians, that the route of the jersey woolmen crossed the Bollin at Styal, by the bridle path at the N end of Quarry Bank mill. If they were simply bringing work to Wilmslow this seems a rather out of the way route to take from the direction of Yorkshire. However there is another suggestion that woollen materials were actually transported by saltmen, who carried salt from the Cheshire wyches to Yorkshire and who found the caves at Styal useful for storage; this would fit in with a route over Lindow Moss suggested by the name Saltersley Hall Farm."

Boundaries

Lindow lies on the edge of two ancient parishes, Wilmslow and Mobberley, and immediately north of a third, Alderley. Mobberley is often quoted as the biggest parish in England. Wilmslow was a pretty big parish too, when it included Alderley Edge.

The boundary between Wilmslow and Mobberley runs north-south across the bog, leaving Lindow at Burleyhurst Bridge in the north and Lindow End in the south. It follows the Sugar Brook for a while, then the line of Boundary Lane which connects Eccups and Rotherwood, but then runs ruler-straight and due south from Lizzie's hut* to the back of The Yews. The straight bit probably was drawn with a ruler on the map across no-man's land, like many of the State boundaries in the USA and Canada.
*See 'Lizzie' chapter.

The parishes and their boundaries were organised in early medieval times, but many of them are much older than that, even pre-Christian, representing ancient tribal and family frontiers. Church sites are often ancient too. Marton church is a spectacular example, standing on its Bronze Age Tumulus. These three churches too probably stand on sites of ancient significance: Wilmslow on its Low or Tumulus by the river crossing, Alderley at a nexus of paths in a big circular space which the A34 curves to avoid, Mobberley by an older monastery site, and oddly not in any village centre.

MH

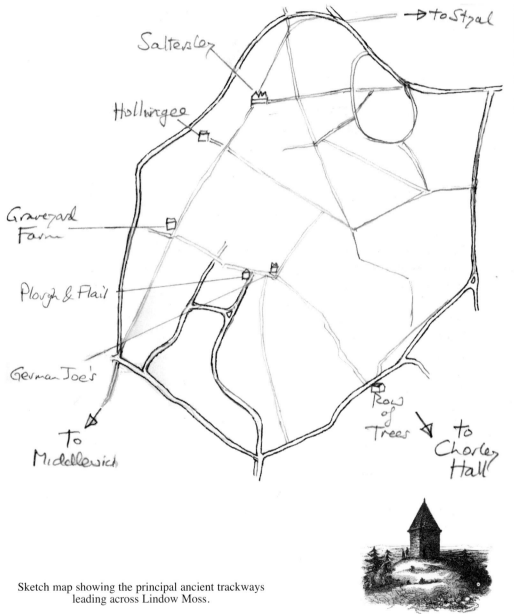

To Styal

Saltersley

Hollingee

Graveyard Farm

Plough & Flail

German Joe's

To Middlewich

Row of Trees

To Chorley Hall

Sketch map showing the principal ancient trackways
leading across Lindow Moss.

The Beacon, Alderley Edge

Significant sighting points in the local landscape:
Above: a distant view of the mound upon which Mottram Church is built and, left, the church and graveyard.
Below: Two great landscape follies. Left, the unmistakable outline of Mow Cop and right, Lyme Cage.

Ancient ways - green lanes of Lindow. Above, leading off Newgate, and below, to Strawberry Lane.

4
Saltersley Hall

Saltersley

'It seems strange for a solid stone house to have been built away from everywhere, with nothing but spongy moss in front and by its sides. Begirt as it is by the quaking bog ...... it may one day go down quick in to the pit, leaving only corpse-lights to flicker o'er the moss where once had been a human home'.   Fletcher Moss Pilgrimages no 2

Strangely isolated even today, at the end of the long straight trackway called Newgate that leads out from Wilmslow, and another from Burleyhurst Lane and Mobberley, is Saltersley. A lonely house. It is on the edge of the huge ancient parish of Mobberley and on the edge of the great peat bog of Lindow, still hereabouts an entity to be reckoned with. Passers-by are most likely to remember Stella's endearing black pigs rootling about, and her Highland cattle. It stands in an overgrown garden, with seven black and white gables - three at the front, two big ones and a small one at the back and one at the end - on a solid base. It is not big - three rooms down and three up -, nor is it tall.

The strangest thing is that the body of this house, alone of all the houses of Lindow or anywhere near it, is built of stone. Not just any old stone either, but the best ashlar stone blocks, like a church, with a finely moulded string course and beautiful mullioned windows.

What is it doing here? Why should anyone want to live here? How was the stone brought so far from the hills, and why?

Saltersley is clearly an important place, holding in some way a key to Lindow. It is built on a sand peninsula, almost surrounded by the bog. This would have provided a perfect defence, because not only would it be hard to approach near, it would be difficult even to find. The sand bank would have provided a healthy place to live in a place that was distinctly unhealthy, and most importantly a well sunk here would provide good clean water, as it did until very recently.

The name is a first clue to its importance. Salt was a vital commodity, traded over wide distances, because it was essential to preserve food. There are well-known salt ways from the salt towns of Cheshire into Lancashire and Derbyshire, often marked by salt names. Saltersley was probably a staging post on an important route, or at a meeting point of two routes. All this is examined in the Trackways chapter.

Why was stone used, and where did it come from? The other old houses in the area are all of brick, except for Row of Trees house which is timber-framed round its brick chimney stack. There are good oak timbers in the roof of Saltersley, and its many gables were all timber-framed as well. Oak would have to be brought from the forest, which was probably only half a mile or so to the north by the Bollin.

Brick making in Cheshire is generally thought to have become common practice after about 1550. Saltersley is older than that.

.   Good stone, freestone that can be cut into ashlar blocks, is only to be had in a few places. The best known source is at Alderley Edge, three miles or so away. Church Quarry, behind the Wizard Inn on top of the Edge, is thought to have provided the stone for the old church of St Mary's at Alderley. The drag for taking it down the hill is still there; called Artist's Lane though that is not what the quarrymen would have called it.

Bringing stone from Alderley to Saltersley would have meant bringing it across the moss, which would be a hazardous undertaking even now and surely impossible 500 years ago. The local tradition is that the Saltersley stone came from not from Alderley but from the Bollin valley at Styal. The story is that Mobberley church is built of stone from Styal, which was carried via Saltersley.

We thought this an unlikely story, so we went in some trepidation to Quarry Bank Mill. The name gives the game away, but the stone here seems to be disappointingly red and friable, good for retaining walls but not for Saltersley or Mobberley Church. Further along the river bank towards Wilmslow a tiny declivity is marked on the map, signed as 'old quarry' by the National Trust. As soon as we reached this the story fell into place. It is an atmospheric spot, heavily tree-grown now, the rock cut into vertical faces with swinging chisel marks. The excellent quality of the stone is easily seen; it is what Alan Garner calls Dimension Stone. It lies under a thin layer of soft red sandy stuff called foxbench, above which is the rougher stuff under the topsoil. The same formation is seen at Church Quarry.

Between the quarry and Mobberley is the Bollin. There does not seem to be a river crossing here. The nearest crossings were by Wilmslow church, or the old packhorse bridge at the other end of the mill. The packhorse bridge route, which is shorter, climbs out of the valley by a deep hollow road, past Bank House farm to the Altrincham Road, then to Morley Green. From here it was probably brought along Eccups Lane to Saltersley, or along Burleyhurst Lane to Mobberley church. But it is possible that, as on the Salt route, Saltersley was the staging post.

It is interesting that, 500 years later, Lizzie Munnerley* walked the same route every day, to Morley Green, Bank House Farm and over the packhorse bridge, to get from her hut by Saltersley to work at Styal Mill.
*See Lizzie chapter.

When was it built? Its architecture points to sometime around 1500, which is the date on the screen at Mobberley church.

1533 is the date of the Mobberley church tower, as recorded on an inscription at its base. John Talbot paid for it and very unusually, the name of the master mason is there too, Richard Plat. The Talbots owned Saltersley in the 16th century, so this seems to offer a confirmation of the connection between the two. If so, was Richard Plat also the master mason at Saltersley? The name Plat, incidentally, probably means Plan. One snag though. The stone of Saltersley is the same as that of the body of the church, but not the tower.

Although it has three equal gables the house is not symmetrical. The present entrances are at the NE end via a modern porch, or via the kitchen lean-to at the back. The old entrances are at the other end, both front and back marked by huge stone lintels - how did they get them here? - and beautifully moulded jambs. At the back of the house is a huge stone stack, with a rather measly brick chimney on top. It looks as though there was another big stack at the SW end, marked by a brick scar today, and there is a small corner chimney at the SE corner.

Entering today via the kitchen nothing makes sense at first. The old stone wall is inside now, between the kitchen and the living room, its beautiful mullioned window unglazed. Here there is a corner fireplace, modern but presumably replacing something older, and a modern staircase. In the middle of the house is a big dark room with a massive stone fireplace which must belong to the big stack we saw outside.

Fletcher Moss visited Saltersley in 1901 and describes this room:

".... there is a long old-fashioned table within that is dated 1639, so the house must have been built before then, or built around the table. Certainly the table cannot be got out of the house without pulling some of the walls down, or it would have been sold, for it is valuable."

Fletcher Moss 2 p230

This is prophetic. A section of wall WAS pulled down around the front window, as can be clearly seen. And the table HAS gone. The plot deepens, because the table was last seen in Cheadle Town Hall. Which, when Cheadle had a Town Council, was Abney Hall. Abney in 1901 was the home of James Watts. James Watts is the one called X who accompanied Fletcher Moss on his Pilgrimages, and took all the photographs. So it looks a though it was James Watts who returned, bought the table, knocked down part of the wall to get it out, and took it to Abney. Where is it now?

Beyond this middle room is - aha! says the architectural historian - a wooden-framed passage running across the house from front to back, connecting the old front and back doors. Now it all makes sense! This is the medieval screens passage. The big room in the middle is the house place, not really a great hall because Saltersley is two-story throughout. I have seen this room called in old Inventories just The House. The room at the far end beyond the screens, unheated now since the end stack was taken down, was the old kitchen, or possibly two service rooms called the buttery and pantry. The first room we entered, with the corner fireplace, was the family parlour.

This was the medieval layout. Family at one end, service at the other,with the hall or house place in the middle and a screens between front and back doors between house place and service.

At some stage the two ends have been reversed, why I don't know but it is not an uncommon thing to do. The kitchen is now at the family end and the old kitchen has become a store. The old entrances have been blocked and new ones made at the present kitchen end.

Two stories have gone down in folk memory concerning Saltersley, and a third may well be in the making. The first concerns a daughter of the house who was courted by a gypsy boy off the moss. When she was forced by her family to jilt him he came to the house, blasted a shot at the front door, and cursed the house, saying that no-one there would ever thrive. The mark is supposed to be still there, but we could not see it.

The second is a family tragedy. On an annotated 1909 map Saltersley Farm is shown as belonging to T. Gillibrand. Gillibrand actually lived in the house attached to the side of Saltersley; he was apparently a German. Samuel Harvey was the tenant farmer. His three year old son was drowned in the pit in the yard. Which is filled in now.

Saltersley is now the home of Ralph and Anita Croxall. It was bought by Ralph's family in 1952 when he was 14 for £4,400: house, farm buildings, and 74.25 acres. They dug and carted away the sand to make the lake, which took 20 years. The old road goes through it; a keen walker went straight through it in a diving suit once. Now the property is divided. When old Mr Croxall died he left the farmhouse to Ralph and split the land between his daughter, Stella, and his other son Hughie. It has been the cause of endless strife, and perhaps the stuff of future legend.

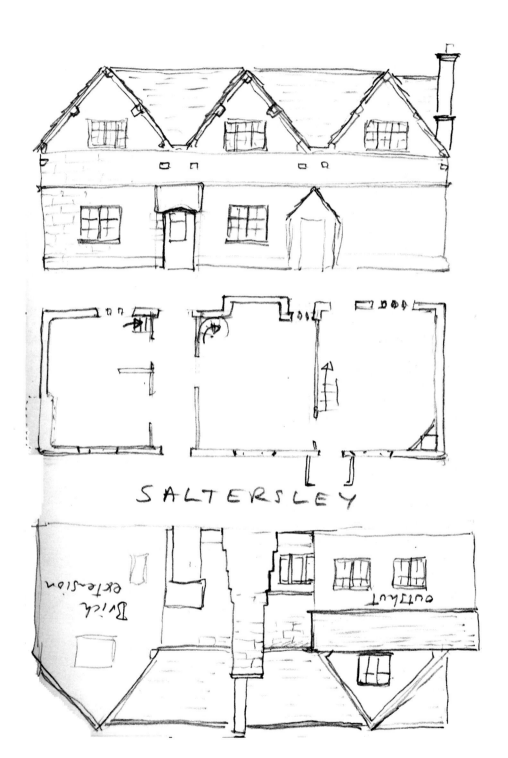

SALTERSLEY

Brick
extension

outshut

The inscription on the tower of Mobberley Church.

Left: The Old Quarry at Styal, which is the most likely source of the stone for both Saltersley Hall and Mobberley Church.

Saltersley Hall, Summer 2002, with Ralph and Anita Croxall

Springfield, Newgate

This is the home of Medical Herbalists Drs Barbara and Kenneth Howe, both in their 80s and both still working. They have 10 acres of moss land, all springy underfoot, made into gardens and paddocks but with the natural bog land flora trying to re-establish itself everywhere.

Their white-painted house was originally two cottages. It has been extended to include a treatment room with a separate entrance. The place gets its name from the wonderful natural spring which fed wells to all the houses in that area of Newgate. Two old residents have extolled its virtues unprompted and bewail the fact that it was 'capped' by the water board when mains water was laid in about 1915. Barbara has uncapped her well and there is a pump. She uses this water for her herbal preparations.

Behind it, on the same plot, is an outhouse, white painted like the main house, which proves to be a complete little bog cottage, charmingly unchanged. It was built in 1822. It has a big black-painted front door and a chimney in one corner. It has not been altered because it is used to store great rows of large labelled jars of Barbara's herbal concoctions. Swallows nest in the beams. It is a one-up one-down cottage, but not as tiny as the one by Maurice Acton's. Downstairs there is a huge old black range in the corner, made in Stockport, and stone flags on the floor. A steep wooden staircase is fitted in the corner. The upstairs room is lit only from the end. Its floor is made of packing case wood - you can read some of the labels from below - with slivers of thin wood over the gaps. There is a lean-to in the yard at the back, by the pump. A small shippon and hayloft are attached to the cottage. The shippon has become a garage, with its end wall knocked out, but the hayloft is complete.

We had a complete tour of the garden, one of the best places to appreciate the quiet beauty that Lindow should possess. They grow their own herbs and also exotic trees. They have had a large pond excavated in the furthest field which needs constant dredging as the peat continues to rise. Finds whilst digging pond include;
A section of PLUTO pipe. The lengths of iron pipe are now stacked up in the hedge.
'The Twig' - An ancient pine tree and its root - now snapped off.
Various old bottles. Flint axe head. Various bits of pottery of which the Char dish, from the Lake District, is the most valuable find.

Christine learnt more about Springfield from Gladys Rogers-Jones (neè Farrington) who lives across the road. Her bungalow is added on to one of the white-painted single-room units that intrigue me so much.

Gladys told us that Springfield had been the home of Mrs Moss and her sons Joby, John and Frank. They ran it as a small holding with a small milk round. It was then bought by a Mr Wright from Mobberley who never intended to live there, just wanted to make a quick profit, which he did by selling it on to Mr Benson(?), who later sold it by auction, when it was bought by the Howes for about £4000. Kenneth was a probation officer and Barbara stood markets selling cloth. She used to set off at 4am and this always woke up the Rogers-Jones's. After retiring from the probation service Kenneth started the homeopathy business and Barbara gave up the textile trade and joined him.

MH

Interior view of the little 1822 bog cottage at Springfield

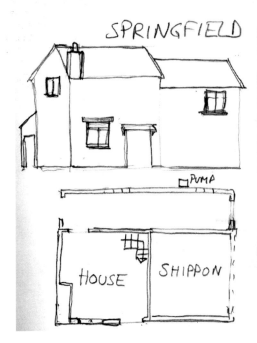

'The Twig' - An ancient pine tree

Above: Barbara Howe and the curious antique diagnostic Pathocast machine.

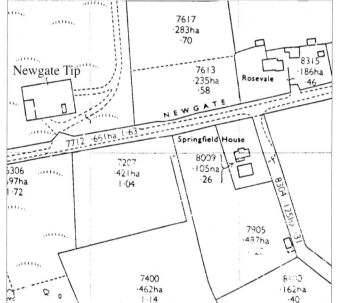

Newgate Tip

7617
·283ha
·70

7613
·235ha
·58

Rosevale

8315
·186ha
·46

NEWGATE

7712 ·661ha 1·63

Springfield House

8009
·105na
·26

7207
·421ha
1·04

6306
·97ha
1·72

8304 ·125ha ·31

7905
·437ha

7400
·462ha
1·14

8400
·162ha
·40

Left: Map of the Newgate area showing the tip, Springfield and Rosevale, the bungalow which was built on the site of Farringtons Farm.

Below: Sketch of Rosevale showing the old wooden barn - one of the original farm buildings, and a tiny section of the original farm house, which was incorporated, at the request of the planning department, into the new bungalow.

white-painted brick   brick   Rosevale   wood   Newgate

Bog Dwellers Not Forgotten

The Crimean Soldiers

The Volunteer Rifle Range, which ran right down the centre of the peat moss, is clearly marked on the Ordnance Survey map of 1844-1899. It was 1000 yards long and stretched across to the vicinity of Platt Cottage, on Greaves Road. Access to the Butts and the wooden platform tower was from Battery Lane. The Rifleman's Arms, a public house on Moor Lane, commemorates all the local Volunteers. What is now known as Rotherwood Road was then called Battery Lane, running from Stormy Point up to the entrance to the peat bog and the rifle range. From that point it turned into Boundary Lane, crossing Newgate and leading to the Wilmslow-Morley boundary. When it reaches Morley it becomes Eccups Lane.

The Crimean War began in 1853 and lasted until 1856. Most of the cottages on Alma Lane date from c1855/56, leading to the assumption that it was named after the Battle of Alma. There is a tale which has proved difficult to verify, although military historians have agreed that it is certainly feasible, that a group of returning Crimean soldiers lived on the moss.

Boys in their early teens - many as young as 14 and the youngest recorded is listed as 12 years old - joined the local Volunteers for the Rifle Brigade. They were sent for drilling, training and target practice to the peat bog, where high stacks of peat had been constructed for the purpose. In 1854 they were sent out to the Crimea as part of the Cheshire Regiment.

Born in Lancashire in 1819, Roger Fenton became the founder and honorary secretary of the Royal Photographic Society in 1853. In 1855 he went out to the Crimea as the world's first war photographer, using wet plates to record the conditions he encountered. No one had ever actually seen visual images of war until Fenton's photographs were published in the Illustrated London News. The young volunteers endured atrocious conditions and witnessed unspeakable horrors. For the first time in history the public at large also had a glimpse of what battlefield combat really entailed.

Those who had survived the war returned home in 1856. Some came back with wounds and medals, but there were others who brought back less honourable souvenirs of their time on the Crimean Peninsula.

These unfortunates were discharged on the grounds of 'ill-health'. This was frequently used as a euphemism for syphilis. Known as the Great Pox, it had been the scourge of the armed forces for centuries. The

Roger Fenton's photograph of Crimean soldiers sharing a drink 1855

CLB

An old photograph of the rifle butts on Lindow Common c1900
An article in a local newspaper dated 26 August 1925 reads as follows:
VOLUNTEER RELIC. Included in the sale of lands at Wilmslow last night was the site of the old
'rifle butts' on the common at Lindow, where the first Cheshire Volunteers and early 'crack shots'
- all members of the Wilmslow, Alderley Edge and Macclesfield Volunteer Corps - learnt to shoot
well. Wilmslow is one of the places where the volunteer movement was first taken up and the local
detachment was for many years part of the old 5th Cheshire Battalion.
Sydney Wheeler collection , courtesy of Wilmslow Historical Society

very word struck dread into the heart and any infected person was a source of infection for those around him. Consequently, the diseased soldiers were not accepted back into their family homes.

Outcast and stigmatised, they ended up back on the peat bog where they had trained, living rough alongside the Bog Warriors. Weaving branches of willow and birch they constructed crude wattle and daub bog huts for themselves, this time using the peat not for target practice, but in the age old tradition, for fuel, cooking and heating.

Bog shelter built of birch withies.

There was rumoured to be a brothel which they frequented on Greaves Road, which runs off Racecourse Road and they bought their drink at the Lomax family home, which backed onto Sandy Lane, close to Greaves Road, and was run as an off licence. This seems to have started a tradition and Sandy Lane became known as the Long Bar. Whatever became of them and where they finally ended up, one can only imagine. By this time the whole area was given a wide berth by 'respectable' people.

"Don't go over the rifle butts
Old bogies there lives in the huts!"

This was a cautionary verse of the period, chanted in the hopes of frightening off the children from playing in the area. Nothing was to happen to improve upon the the bog's bad reputation during the years which followed.

1938 The new Rifleman's Arms stands alongside the original, now awaiting demolition.

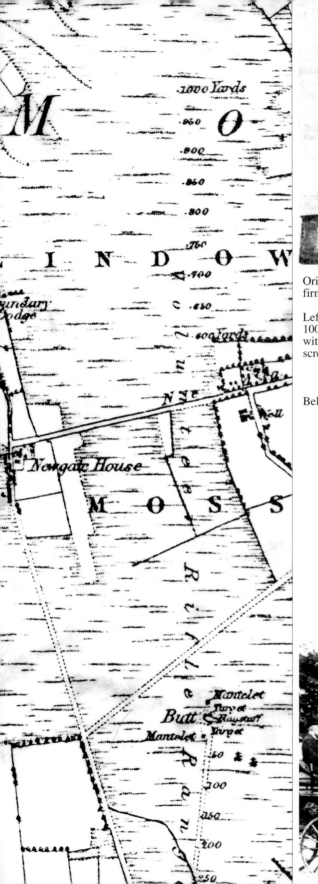

Original metalwork sign made by a Manchester firm for the original pub.

Left: Section from the 1873 map showing the full 1000 yards extent of the Volunteer Rifle Range, with the Butts, Turrets and Mantelets (bullet proof screens) clearly marked

Crown copyrig

Below: Old Rifleman's Arms
Sydney Wheeler collection, courtesy Wilmsl
Historical Socie

Turf Diggers and Irish Paddys

Eddie Bailey ran the turf cutting operations on Saltersley Common and his brother Bill those on Lindow Moss. Bill had a plot leading towards Greaves Road, which is now the tip fill. The Jones family lived next to the tip. Greaves Road is a pleasant green lane, once frequented by the gypsies. It led to two tips - at the top end to Eccups Lane joining Newgate and northwards crossing Altrincham Road to Kings Road, Pownall Hall and the tip which was where the Rugby Club now stands.There are some old cottages and enclosures amongst areas of woodland which are now well fenced to prevent access. A deep ditch runs along one side and nettles and moss now cover the remains of old brick buildings in undergrowth, possibly demolished cottages.

There is large area of well tended allotments belonging to members of Lindow Horticultural Society. From here, through the trees, one can see the huge glass car showroom towering incongruously on the corner of the turn to Morley, and hear the traffic noise from Altrincham Road.

Seven turf rooms ran off Newgate. Each man dug his own room and Mr Farrington, of Farrington's Farm, bought the peat from them when it had dried out. Born in 1908, his daughter Gladys, now aged 94, clearly remembers her childhood days.

"It was the black peat that he bought - it's grey for about the first three feet. Father wanted the black peat, with the fibres in it. He took it round Bowden on the back of a lorry and sold it to all the big houses. When it was stacked to dry the wagtails used to nest in it. I got a good hiding once off my father for disturbing them, I wanted to see inside the nests, look at the eggs. I was about four years old at the time. We used to take a picnic and paddle in Mobberley Brook at Burleyhurst Bridge. It was lovely. There were skylarks and plovers, pheasants and partridge - all wild. And hares. Then it became all polluted with the effluent from the Eccups Lane caravan site. Boundary Farm is now called Cedar Lodge. Rotherwood Road was called Eight Furlongs because it was exactly one mile to Morley Green."

Gladys still lives on Newgate in a bungalow built on the site of Farrington's Farm, which was originally owned by the Traffords. The Farringtons were tenants. Gladys eventually bought the farm and knocked down all but a small section at the front, which is incorporated into the bungalow. The farm, together with most of the other properties along Newgate, was supplied by spring water until the mains were laid c1915 and the well spring was capped.

Eddie brought in a lot of Irish labourers and the Long Bar or Long Tap was a magnet for turf diggers and Irish 'paddys'. The ale was sold in quart jars and the customers used take it outside into Sandy Lane and

The Long Bar, for many years the scene of round the clock drunken revelry. Decent folk gave it a wide berth and warned their children to keep away from the place. The little off licence was half way along, on the right, fronting the Altrincham Road. Now better known as Sandy Lane.

Greaves Road, named after Mr Greaves, who owned the Moss Litter Works. This is an ancient trackway which linked up with the network of paths which traversed the bog between Lindow and Mobberley.

"The Bog Warriors built and lived in all manner of huts, sheds and shelters. You should have seen the Long Bar years ago - the Irish paddy labourers were so drunk - they'd be drunk for weeks. They even slept drunk in hedges. They got through buckets of ale." George Potts

Lindow is still a land of huts, sheds and shelters - here is just a tiny selection of the many that we encountered during our travels around the area!

The Newgate headquarters of the Humane Society. Alongside stands one of the long water troughs, dated 1887, provided by The Ladies' Humane Society. The troughs were placed at strategic sites to enable working horses to quench their thirst.

Above: Always a favourite nesting place for grey wagtails, peat turves stooked for drying on Saltersley Common
Sydney Wheeler collection , courtesy of Wilmslow Historical Society

Right: Interior of the old 'bothy' outbuilding at Hollingee, where "*two casual farm workers, Charlie and George Baguley, used to live. One died of the cold and the other lost his feet from frostbite.*" Later, the dispossessed Mrs Baddeley and her sons lived there, trying to eke out a living by fruit picking. They ended up living on the bog.

Turves laid out to dry in windrows
Sydney Wheeler collection , Wilmslow Historical Society

Extracts from the Personal Reminiscences of Mr Potts, born 1897,
who lives on Lindow Common.

Over the years people have lived in shanties on Lindow. Usually they had a strip of land with a hut and little else. Charlie Moore lived there with his wife and two children until about 1940. Another hut was occupied by Joby Waters. A man named Adshead had an old caravan on the site. It has been said that some supplemented their living by poaching. Organised groups from Wilmslow and Stockport poached from Morley right through to the Tatton Estates. Other people had allotments, 100 yards by 20 yards, which they cultivated and paid a rent of 5/- per year. Close to a house called Bowers Folly is a ridge of land. This was an old sand pit but the sand was poor because it contained layers of peat. Concrete made with this could only be used where appearance did not matter. Mr Greaves built the road which bears his name, and the little railway line which carried peat from the bog to his Moss Litter Works. He had four waggons, each carrying 500 blocks. The were pulled by a donkey engine, then later by a pony. The peat was ground down and used as bedding for horses, instead of straw and was said to be especially beneficial for their feet.

courtesy of Wilmslow Historical Society

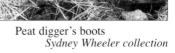

Peat digger's boots
Sydney Wheeler collection

drink. Workers used to take their lunch time 'baggin' there - agricultural labourers, brick layers and itinerant tinkers were sprawled along the whole length of the track, supping their ale. In the summertime there were hundreds of them. They put their jugs and bottles in the heather to keep cool. The off-licence was eventually acquired by Boddington's brewery and was closed down as soon as the Boddington Arms was up and running.

If the Long Bar was regarded by polite Victorian society as a nursery of vice, the Black Donkey, round the corner in Greaves Road, a small ale house which offered additional pleasures, was the open university. By this time the peat bog had become the sink of human misery and the ultimate destination of its inhabitants was either the Workhouse opposite Lindow Common or the one at Arclid.

Eddie Bailey's house was called Malvern and stood on the corner of Morley Road and Sandy Lane. He used to dip the peat turves in in an old bath tub of diesel oil and paraffin mixture and then sell them as fire lighters, going from house to house by horse and cart.

Other bog characters from the early part of the twentieth century include Fred Shepherd, who lived in the sand holes. He used to go around knocking on doors, holding out a great big jam jar and demanding it be filled with tea.

Sam Jackson and his children, Eric and Marion, tenanted Hollingee before moving to Graveyard Farm. Two casual farm workers, Charlie and George Baguley, used to live in the old 'bothy' outbuilding at Hollingee. One died of the cold and the other lost his feet from frostbite. Constantine lived with a goat under Burleyhurst Bridge and some thought he might be a spy.

Originally a Trafford house, Platt Cottage, on Greaves Road, has been in the Potts family since it was built in 1850. Originally held on a peppercorn rent, George Potts finally purchased it outright.

"Joby Waters was a poacher who lived next door to Platt Cottage. He made his living at it. In those days the whole area was full of turf rooms and hawkers. There were two brothers, Lenny and Charlie Adshead. They built and lived permanently in a clod shelter. Lenny hawked peat and vegetables from a horse and cart. The Bog Warriors built and lived in all manner of huts, sheds and shelters. You should have seen the Long Bar years ago - the Irish paddy labourers were so drunk - they'd be drunk for weeks. They even slept drunk in hedges. They got through buckets of ale. The Romanys were all right, but the Irish tinkers spelt trouble. They were a pest. There would be up to a hundred Gypsies around here at any one time."

On the corner between Greaves Road and the Long Bar are two interesting enclosures, apparently unloved and unused for a long time. The hedges are very ancient and old fruit trees were in blossom in April 2002. I suspect that this was Cabbage Mary's, who 'looked like a gypsy and grew fruit and veg which she sold at the gate'. In the 1920s the bog dwellers' children were sent to buy produce from her.

There was also Black Tom, who lived rough on Ikey's (Isaac's) Moss. Farmer George Spragg got annoyed with Black Tom when he let his goats onto the Lindow Farm land and overgrazed the fields. At one time there were 42 children living on the bog including the Elams, Burgesses, Whittakers and Frosts.

The Baddeley family consisted of a mother with two sons. The mother eventually married a widower and when he died the children from his original marriage threw them out. Suddenly homeless, they moved into a shippon at Hollingee and tried to support themselves by fruit picking. They ended up living in a caravan on the bog.

George Spragg's daughter, Mabel, looked out of the bedroom window at Lindow Farm one day and saw the two sons digging a grave on the bog, just in front of the caravan. The Spraggs alerted the police who came and removed the dead mother's body. The police car got stuck in the bog when they tried to drive it away to the mortuary, a tribulation which appears to have caused some considerable mirth at Lindow Farm.

Mr Richardson built a little brick place, backing onto Newgate, to house his family. The Richardson's eventually sold this small house to Miss Lucius, a 'theatrical person' from Didsbury, and at one period she rented it out to Peter Goodright, the impressionist. The property was then bought by Peter Rainbird, who later confessed to the murder of his Spanish wife, who had 'left' her husband and the home many years previously*.

*See 'A Place of Sacrifice' chapter.

The Home Guard stored molotov cocktails under Burleyhurst Bridge. Some of the schoolboys used to pinch them and take them to the Saltersley sand hole to explode. One septuagenarian still remembers the burns he received to his legs and wellingtons when a molotov cocktail was thrown towards him. It exploded at his feet.

Between The Wars

The 1930s was a time of great social and political unrest. By the middle of this decade the Saltersley end of Newgate had attracted some strange bedfellows. Where else would one find such a disparate gathering of families? On the land where The Brackens now stands was an old bow topped Gypsy caravan, with steep wooden steps. This was home to Mr and Mrs Ryder, who were 'elderly'. Mr Ryder had a small moss room on the Greaves Road side of Newgate. Parked alongside this towering edifice was an old bus, where Mr and Mrs Holden and their two children, Clifford and Violet resided. Eventually they were to build a 'very basic' bungalow, which in later years was extended to become The Brackens. Clifford became an active communist and went to fight in the Spanish Civil War.

On a piece of wasteland by the roadside, where Rotherwood crosses Newgate and continues towards Morley, yet another old charabanc housed the Marshes, a family of fascists. This was next door to the Richardson's small brick built house, built by Mr Richardson himself in a determined effort to improve the fortunes of his family. The Levines, a Jewish family from Manchester, lived next door to the Richardsons in a small wooden bungalow. Following the outbreak of war in 1939 the Levines returned to Manchester. Mrs Levine was a large breasted woman and her great howls of anguish echoed round Newgate when her nipple got stuck in the old wooden mangle when they were struggling to load it into removal van!

In the meantime the farmers' wives were rushing to join the Primrose League, which met at the Conservative Hall on Kennerleys Lane, and was the forerunner of the Young Conservatives.

In 1939 Walter Stansby, owner of the Rex Buildings and a fascist supporter, invited Oswald Mosley - (OE Mos=peat bog + leah=wood: Oxford Names Companion) - to hold a rally in the Rex Cinema. The forthcoming event was well publicised. On 25 August 1939 the local Advertiser carried an announcement that the film of the week showing at the Rex Cinema was "Keep On Smiling", starring Miss Gracie Fields, together with notice that the British Union of Fascists would be holding a rally at the cinema on Sunday, 14 November 1939.

War was declared on 3 September 1939 and feelings were running high during the intervening weeks between this advance notice and the event itself. Admission was strictly by invitation only and drew fascist supporters from a wide area. Travelling by coaches and taxis, they arrived in large numbers to hear their leader speak. A heavy presence of Mosley's brownshirts patrolled the entrance steps of the Rex Cinema.

For the first time in its political history Wilmslow rebelled and the huge outcry quickly degenerated into open fighting. When the angry crowd overturned a bus loaded with Mosley supporters the police were called to break up the ensuing fracas. Injuries were inflicted on both sides and Mosley was eventually smuggled out of the Rex Buildings through one of the back exits. In 1940 Walter Stansby was interned at Port Erin, in the Isle of Man, for the duration of the war.

Just off Newgate, on the bridle path which eventually becomes

Eccups Lane, is the headquarters of the Humane Society. Alongside stands one of the long water troughs provided by The Ladies' Humane Society, founded in 1887 to prevent animal suffering. These huge troughs were placed at strategic sites in the towns and cities to enable the poor overworked cart and dray horses to quench their thirst.

Present Times

Old men who have hard and difficult lives, labouring amongst the peat and sand diggings, speak wistfully of the departed ground nesting birds whose presence they enjoyed and respected. The skylarks, curlews, corncrakes, partridges and pheasants are all gone now, their habitats destroyed.

There are both good and bad things to remember about the old days. Bronchitic old men still expectorated on the pavements in the 1940s and 1950s and there were 'No Spitting' signs on the old North Western buses. Penalty £5. There were also the shell shocked war veterans who could not stop shaking and trembling. Useless and unwanted, they stood for hours on the street corners with nowhere else to go.

Now incorporated in SK9, one of the most sought after and costly post codes in the country, this period of local history has become conveniently erased from modern recorded history, a fact which still provokes a chuckle from elderly locals with longer memories.

Around the edges and especially in the sand hills there are still reminders - handmade bricks in the undergrowth, surviving garden plants, bits of corrugated iron roofing, gutters and chimney pipes, broken window glass and bits of pottery, a few kitchen artifacts rusting just beneath the surface. The last bog dwelling was demolished in 1971.

One can still see the inheritance of the Bog Warriors today. Around the fringes are livery and riding stables, boarding kennels, a car breaker's yard, tree nurseries, garden centres and other horticultural operations. What must have begun as pathetic little livelihoods for marginalised folk have gradually been developed into thriving businesses. There are a number of small caravan parks and static sites, now smart and well maintained.

The Bog Warriors are long gone, and almost forgotten. Around the northern edges of the peat diggings the humble moss cottages and wooden shacks of yesteryear have gradually been transformed and are virtually unrecognisable - unless you know what to look for. Those long narrow strips of garden hold the clue. They started out as moss rooms.

CP

6
The Gypsies

The Gypsies

Lindow Common is one of the flagship conservation sites of Macclesfield Borough Council. It was designated a national Site of Special Scientific Interest (SSSI) in 1963 and a Local Nature Reserve (LNR) in 1987, supported by the Countryside Commission and English Nature. However, it is Racecourse Road, which surrounds Lindow Common in an almost complete circle, which brings us to historically more interesting territory. It may also hold the clue as to why Alderman John Royle saw fit to buy the Common and donate it to the residents of Wilmslow.

Exactly eight furlongs - one mile - in length, the racecourse was a dirt track circuit used for horse racing. It had been created by the Gypsies, to enable them to put their horses through their paces and show off their mettle. Their horse trading was conducted around Lindow Common, drawing people in from the surrounding areas. There was even a wooden stand for spectators, erected at the finishing line.

According to Earwalker: *"In front of the workhouse is the Racecourse, where races are held during the Wakes, the last week in August. These races, which are of a very inferior character, do much harm to the neighbourhood and are in a fair way of being permanently discontinued"*.

Not exactly the sport of kings. This was Lindow's version of Appleby Fair and, as far as the local burgesses were concerned, the horse races attracted unruly and undesirable elements. By 1896 the Gypsies' racing days were numbered.

"Many years ago a Local Committee unsuccessfully endeavoured to get absolute control of Lindow Racecourse, after which the Wilmslow Urban District Council took the matter in hand, supported by a monstre Petition from the Ratepayer's Association, containing 1500 signatures. The petition was duly forwarded to the legal advisers of the lords of the Manor, accompanied by a letter from the Council asking for an interview on the question, which request was granted. The Council appointed a Deputation ...... we met on the 5th day of October 1896. ... the Council finally suggested terms which were accepted. Hence the question which had so long agitated the public mind was for ever settled.

At a Special meeting of the Council on the 5th day of March 1897, a letter was read out by Mr E H Prior, Assistant Clerk, from John Royle Esq, of Northwood, Wilmslow, containing an offer to pay the purchase money for the land, and present the same to the inhabitants of Wilmslow to be used as a Recreation Ground for ever. The Common has been enclosed by private subscription, and can now be protected from all encroachments."

Andrew Pearson 'Wilmslow Past & Present' 1897.

Opposite: The Pattison family, 31 July 1927   *courtesy Thomas Ward*

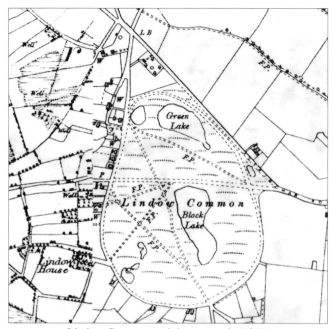

Lindow Common and the racetrack c1844.
The narrow moss rooms are also clearly visible on the left of the common,
running towards the peat bog.

Crown copyright

Amos Smith and family at Workhouse Farm c1920

courtesy Stella Willett

By amazing coincidence this coup was pulled off just in of time for Queen Victoria's Diamond Jubilee on June 22 1897, celebrated in Wilmslow with huge processions, brass bands, fireworks and the gifting of Lindow Common - historically common land - by the great and the good to the residents of Wilmslow! The monument commemorating this great event was erected in the centre of the very spot where the Gypsies had always camped. It is still there.

I have asked many elderly local residents whether they remember the Gypsies and the question always evokes the same response - a combination of affection, wistfulness and curiosity about colourful characters with a way of life long gone. One Newgate resident remembers her mother's tales. *"One Gypsy had a bear called Venus and he went to Congleton with it at fair time. About 1895, not long before they were turned off. That Councillor got himself on the plaque when they re-opened the Common. That's good, it was never closed!"*

Gypsies had come to Lindow Moss since the Middle Ages - some itinerant, but many settling permanently in the network of 'green lanes' which criss cross the region. They became part of the local landscape. Mainly of Welsh origin, the Gypsies gathered at Delamere and travelled to Lindow in convoy. They were *"black as berries, hair and skin"*, and lived in the traditional horse drawn bow topped vans. Upon arrival the first thing they did was to run chicken netting round the van and let the hens out.

After dark they set their horses to graze in adjacent fields and took them out at first light. If you got up early enough you could catch them! They galloped their horses round the Common, where many had set up camp. They were not merely passing through, they stayed there permanently,. There was also a traditional stopping site on Morley Green.

The Gypsies lived in all the green lanes around Morley and Wilmslow. Strawberry Lane, Gore Lane, Hard Hill at the top of Moor Lane - they were all full of Romany caravans, some permanent, some transient. At the top of Racecourse Road is Greaves Road, which is still a green lane. This was also a camping place for the Gypsies.

Built in 1773 the Workhouse stood on Altrincham Road, facing Lindow Common. After its closure it was run as a tenanted farm, shared by two families. During the 1920s Gypsy Amos Smith and his family lived as tenants at Workhouse Farm, alongside George and Bertha Brown. Bertha was also a Brown (unrelated) before her marriage and her father, Levi Brown, started Brown's the Builders at the Rookery, near the station.

Their granddaughter, Stella Willett, was the last person to be born at Workhouse Farm and she still recalls the stories her grandmother told her. From the 1860s-1880s Granny Bertha used to visit the old Gypsy

Queen on the Common. Held in great reverence, she sat on the steps of her van smoking a clay pipe, dispensing free advice and selling herbal cures and ointments.

Cyril Wood, of Newgate, clearly remembers Amos, who married his great aunt. He obviously made a lasting impression on the young boy: *"Old Amos was a big, handsome fellow. He dealt in horses. When he died my mother said she'd never seen so many Rolls Royces as there were at his funeral. They came from everywhere. Young Amos, his son, worked for Masseys in Alderley Edge. He married Marion Woods and they had two daughters. The Gypsy men always stood stock still, arms folded across their chest, just watching. When all the locals were skating on Black Lake, one Gypsy fellow used to stand at the edge, watching us. Only his eyes moved. They loved brass and copper. Inside the vans there was brass everywhere. Horse brasses and suchlike.*

The Gypsy Taylors camped near the Boddington Arms. My brother, Norman, used to play there with them. They've ruined it round here now. Skylarks, plovers, corncrakes, pheasant and partridge, hares - all gone. I used to love listening to the skylarks and corncrakes."

The Boddington Arms is built on a triangular piece of land which was previously known as the Flat Iron Field, due to its shape. This was also a favourite stopping place for the Gypsies and it was here that the men cut and fashioned withies of willow and birch to make clothes pegs, whilst the women went off to the local tips. One was down Kings Road and is now the site of the Rugby Club. Another was down Strawberry Lane. From these tips the women collected empty sardine tins, which they cleaned before cutting the metal into thin bands with which to bind the wooden pegs. When the Gypsy women called round hawking their pegs they were treated kindly by local residents, some giving them "a crust for the baby" or cast-off children's clothing, and paying 4d per dozen for the pegs.

It is easy to imagine their presence in the green lanes, still and silent now. One can almost hear the distant voices and the sounds of their horses and smell the wood and peat smoke of their night fires. Gypsy children gathering medicinal herbs from the hedgerows, the vital ingredients for Her Majesty's cures, whilst their mothers sold fortunes and pegs and potions door to door. The men, meanwhile, were busy conducting their horse trading activities.

Gypsies also lived on what is now a small tree plantation at the very top of Moor Lane, beyond Ned Yates Garden Centre. There was another encampment near to what is now the Horticon site, where they used to set up camp in a huge circle on a bank, the horses tethered nearby.

Saltersley is so named because the men bringing salt from the

Cheshire brine pits used to stop there overnight to change horses. It was the Gypsies who supplied fresh ones, taking the salter's exhausted pack horses in exchange and restoring them to soundness. For a long time Saltersley was principally a horse trading post.

The outbreak of war in September 1939 brings us to Lindow Farm. The introduction of rationing quickly put paid to travellers and itinerants. To obtain a ration book one needed a permanent address. Many vagabonds and tinkers were taken to the Arclid Workhouse. Others, squatting in huts and shelters around the margins of Lindow Moss, were re-housed by the local authorities.

Since Lindow historically belonged to the Gypsies, or vice versa, the Manchester authorities rounded up 39 families and sent them to Lindow, in the mistaken belief that that was from whence they had come. A Romany family usually consists of three generations, so this was quite a lot of people.

The fields in question sloped steeply down - the land was part of a sand hill and useless for grazing. Prior to the outbreak of war Stretford Motor Cycle Club used it for scrambling, but in October 1939 there was a knock at the farm door. Three Gypsy men handed farmer George Spragg a note from the Inspector of Police in Manchester. The note said "Mr Spragg, you are to take 39 families and you will receive 2/- per week ground rent for each family."

The fields were to be requisitioned. Romanys, compelled this time, returned to Lindow.

George Spragg's daughter Mabel grew up at Lindow Farm and has clear memories of the families who lived alongside them for the duration of the second world war.

"Water was fetched from the well pump. The Gypsies were given ration books like everyone else, but their cooking was done in the traditional way. They made open air camp fires, with a 'chitty box' from which was suspended the old black cauldron pots containing boiling bacon - making huge soups. The only nuisance caused was some damage to the boundary hedges by the taking of wood for the fires. The horses were tethered on the lower slopes of the fields."

One of the families was that of Doris Shaw, a niece of the well known Collins fairground family. Tragically, her ten year old son died of meningitis and was given a Gypsy funeral during which their caravan, together with all its contents, was burnt. No longer classified as 'travellers', the bereaved family, presumably free to leave, walked away never to return.

Three generations lived in each bow-topped van. The old men slept under an awning erected alongside, also in sling hammocks strung underneath the vans. When the war ended they took to the road once more, leaving in dribs and drabs. Many made their way into Wales, others went down south.

An ex-Eton schoolmaster, Bower Alcock, built and lived at Bowers Folly, on Greaves Road. His friend was a barrister, Herwald Morris. In the 1950s, in an attempt to rid Morley Green of Gypsies they pulled a bluff by erecting a notice saying 'No Movable Dwellings Allowed Here. Anyone Disobeying this Notice will be Fined'. There was, in fact, no existing law under which anyone could be prosecuted, but they were still being harassed.

Some went to the Middlewich area. True Romanys, but no longer free to roam, they are now owner occupiers on their own controlled site. Mabel took me to visit them. The site is designed and owned by Mr Price. He began with an existing bungalow and a small piece of land, purchased from an elderly lady, plus an additional six acres, purchased in stages from the farmer.

Clean and well maintained, it stands alongside the busy Middlewich-Sandbach road, opposite the canal. There are about thirty Roma vans, brick built toilet blocks and mains electricity to each van. Water is fetched from outside taps in traditional Romany water carriers. Settled in one place, they appear to have combined the best of the new without sacrificing their traditional ways.

Seventeen year old Hawthorn (*'after my grandfather'*) James Price leads a typical Romany life. He was busily preparing for Appleby Fair in June, his newly painted 'sulky' ready for the big race. The horses, of which they have 100, some at grass at other sites in the area, are his abiding passion. He took me to see some of them.

The Collier, a beautiful seven year old cob stallion, is Hawthorn's pride and joy. His name seems to refer to pit ponies. Amongst Romany horse traders The Collier is rated the best stud in the whole country and is never short of work. Mr Price has turned down astronomical offers for The Collier. In the next box was his two year old son, bred by Hawthorn.

None of the horses wore head collars. Hawthorn just put a thin piece of rope round their necks and led them out to meet me. The Collier did a bit of frisking around because in an adjoining field three mares were calling to him. Newly arrived from London on the previous day, they awaited his services. Next I was introduced to another yearling. a three-quarter bred trotter called The Champ. A further 15 yearlings, currently at grass in Northwich, will also be going to Appleby Fair. Hawthorn also has ferrets, fighting cocks, a fine lurcher bitch, a crossed Staffordshire bull terrier pup, and caged birds. Four litters of young kittens tumbled around together in the hedgerows.

Thomas Ward and his wife invited me into their caravan to watch a video of Appleby Fair. Thomas is descended from the Pattison family, of Doncaster. His grandmother was Violet Morrison, his aunt Chris Pattison. His great grandfather was George Pattison, seen in the photograph with his wife Janie and family. George's brother was known as Crying Tommy Pattison - a famous bare knuckle fighter and Thomas proudly produced a book about the Pattison fighters.

In her 80s and failing, his mother has her own large Roma van alongside that of the family, who provide round the clock care. Elderly Gypsies don't end up in nursing homes."No one else is going to look after my Mum." said Thomas, explaining why they would be missing Appleby Fair this year.

The Ward family moved to Mr Price's site after 23 years in Winsford. *"We're very happy here. Mr Prices's site is much nicer. It's well maintained and there's no rubbish anywhere. It's one of the finest."*

Although his mother Tilly was one of the Gypsy Smiths, writer and broadcaster the Reverend Bramwell Evans - 'Romany' - moved to Wilmslow simply because it was convenient for commuting to the BBC studios in Manchester. Having expounded so much effort in discouraging any Romany presence in the town, it is perhaps an irony that 'Romany's' Caravan now stands in pride of place outside Wilmslow Library.

CP

Typical willow clothes peg
with tin binding, c1930

Traditional Romany steel water carrier.

Three generations of the Pattison Family c1895. The small girl sitting on the steps of the vardo is the grandmother of Thomas Ward.

courtesy Thomas Ward

Bridle path leading to Pownall Hall, 1920s. This was once a continuation of Greaves Road, crossing the Altrincham Road and leading to the tip, a favourite haunt of the Lindow Gypsies. Now Kings Road.

courtesy Stella Willett

The Gypsies are gone. This photograph of the old workhouse dates from the winter of 1897, just a few months after the enclosure of the common and the erection of the stone monument to mark the occasion.

Sydney Wheeler collection, courtesy Wilmslow Historical Society

The Gypsies are back! A poor quality 1950s photograph of Gypsy Taylor at an encampment on Morley Green. This was around the time that Bowyer Alcock and his barrister friend, Herwald Morris were erecting their posters.

courtesy Cyril Bradley

Lindow Farm, home of the Spragg family for many years and also, for the duration of the second world war, a holding camp for Manchester's Gypsies.

Finding themselves in Yorkshire at the outbreak of war, the Pattison family were forced to abandon their travelling lifestyle for the duration and moved into a large house in Bradford. The lady sitting and holding the small child is Violet Pattison, Thomas Ward's great grandmother. His mother, Emily Ward is standing behind, second from the left.

courtesy Thomas Ward

Appleby Horse fair June 1938
Left to right: Peggie Mowett, Jackie Moore with his wife Sara and children Peggie, Esther, Saidie, George and Jackie. Also Esther Ward and Chrissy and Jane Pattison.

The annual Appleby Horse Fair, which always takes place in June, is an important event in the Gypsy calendar. Romanys travel from all over the country to attend, some setting off weeks beforehand. Travelling in the old way, with horse drawn vans, they can only cover 20 miles per day. This huge fair has been held every year in living memory - except for 2001, when, like every other livestock event, it had to be cancelled due to the foot and mouth outbreak. As a consequence the 2002 fair attracted huge numbers of travellers and their horses. Pictured here are scenes from the Appleby Fair in the 1930s
courtesy Thomas Ward

Appleby Fair, Appleby   27938

May 2002. Hawthorn James Price with prize winning stallion The Collier,
the darling of Appleby Fair.

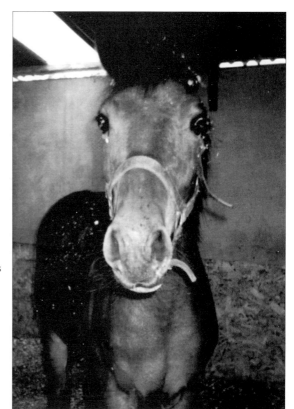

A lovely Gypsy yearling.
The Champ, a threequarter bred trotter, is
ready to make an appearance at this
year's Appleby Fair.

Below: Modern Gypsies - Mr and Mrs
Thomas Ward at Three Oaks,
Middlewich.

7
Little
Settlements

Little Settlements

Paddock Hill

Almost imperceptible at ground level, Paddock Hill can be seen quite clearly on an aerial photograph. It follows a similar contour to the mound behind Graveyard Farm and the two are in alignment, connected by an ancient footpath which crosses the moss, linking the two sites. The footpath then continues across Hollingee land to Saltersley. This may also have been the location of a neighbouring Iron Age settlement.

Now one of the most pleasant, sought after and expensive areas to live, in the old days Paddock Hill was pig country. Most of the cottages had wells and ponds and every cottager had a moss room and kept at least one pig. The narrow moss rooms and tiny enclosures where pigs once rootled for acorns and beech mast are landscaped gardens now, or have smart paddock fencing to contain horses and small ponies for the children.

The original Forest Charter was granted on 6th November 1217, by Henry III. Salted meat formed a vital and significant part of the medieval diet and the Charter granted to the rural population the rights of mast (nuts and other forest fruits) and pannage (pasturage of swine) in addition to those of turbary (digging of turf and peat).

The oldest cottages are set back from the winding metalled road which runs from Knutsford Road to Paddock Hill, on a narrow half moon shaped lane which may have formed part of the original route. Just before one reaches this little backwater, where the lane forks left into Clay Lane, leading to Moss Lane, Mobberley, there is a fenced triangular area which contains a deep and swampy pond, with an old wooden board marked 'Danger!'. This is probably a lingering remnant of the original moss.

One of the earliest properties on the half moon is Holford. Originally a thatched moss cottage turned smallholding, Holford was built at a right angle to the lane and incorporates what is reputed to be the smallest house in the county, which is also set at right angles, leading one to wonder if they were sited on a trackway which no longer exists. This ancient little cottage, just 10 feet square, is situated across from the main dwelling, on the opposite side of the entrance. It remains exactly as it was, with blue lime washed plaster and a minute upper floor and appears to have had its own separate narrow moss room which runs parallel to Holford's own. Judging from the surviving remnants of boundary hedging the Holford land now appears to encompass three moss rooms. Matthew will tell us more.

CP

Opposite: Alfred Acton c1940, peeling potatoes outside Holford . courtesy Maurice Acton

Alfred Acton re-thatching
Holford c1950

courtesy Maurice Acton

Holford newly thatched c1950

courtesy Maurice Acton

Maurice and *"the weeniest bog house that can be imagined."*

Sketch showing the stages of Holford's development

HOLFORD

Holford 2002

Holford

This is Maurice Acton's house at Paddock Hill. The white-painted cottage stands at right angles to the road, with a jumble of outhouses beyond it and a bit of garden sloping down to become a moss room. Attached to the cottage at the end away from the road is a little shippon for four cows, with a hayloft above with the characteristic ventilating holes in the brickwork. Everything is still there. The house is a two-up, two-down with a narrow staircase in the middle between the two rooms. Maurice remembers it as a thatched house with much lower eaves and the bedrooms tucked up in the thatch and only lit from the ends.

Holford evidently grew in stages. First came the little thatched cottage on the edge of the bog. Then a shippon was built on to the end of it. Then the cottage was reconstructed with higher eaves and a tiled roof.

Next to the cottage is the weeniest bog house that can be imagined. Only ten foot square, but of brick with an upstairs and a downstairs and a chimney. One up one down, with a ladder to the upper floor. Fireplace and copper. A lean-to next to it is the outside toilet.

Walking down onto Maurice's Moss room is a good way to get the bog atmosphere. It stretches a long way but is only narrow, with thorn hedges on either side. Part way down is a primeval pool, with a sinister willow tree cracking up and falling into it. Beyond that the moss room splits into two even narrower ones, so either the Holford one was split into two at some stage, or two older ones were joined together to make one.

MH

Next door to Holford is Lea House. Originally a farm where up to a hundred pigs were kept, Lea House also incorporated a small abbatoir. In later years this practice was abandoned and the pigs were sent to Chelford Market for sale and slaughter.

Most of these old cottages originally had earthen floors. All the bricks were made at the brick field down nearby Folly Lane, so called because of the danger from flying bricks! Each householder built his own cottage with hand made bricks from clay which he had dug from his little patch. The clay was trundled to the brick yard, where it was exchanged for bricks already made for someone else's clay, and so it went on.

Alf Acton, Maurice's uncle, was a pig slaughterer. During the second world war, when rationing was introduced, Alf was farming pigs at the Row of Trees. Officially one was only permitted to slaughter one pig a year. With a wink and a nod from Alf, pig meat was handed out in brown paper parcels to the local constables, a routine which continued on a regular basis for years before suspicions were eventually aroused and a directive arrived from the Ministry. Alf Acton was to be checked out by a policeman from the neighbouring Wilmslow station. Alf, however, was ahead of him.

By the time Mrs Acton opened the door to the constable Alf was tucked up in bed, pretending to be ill. The constable insisted on going upstairs to the bedroom to check for himself. Under the covers, alongside Alf, was a dead pig, already drawn and quartered. Alf later moved to Vost Farm, which was later to become The Cheshire Smokehouse.

Ernest Acton was born at Paddock Hill, just next door to Maurice Acton in 1923. They are distant cousins. When Ernest was two years old his family moved to a cottage at the top end of Moor Lane and he spent most of his childhood playing around Saltersley Common. He remembers most of the old poachers and agricultural labourers who were around then. By that time Black Tom had exchanged his tent of yesteryear for an old caravan which was sited near Lindow Farm. He lived in it with his brother and, of course, the goats. Both brothers were inveterate poachers, as were the gypsies, and they all sold their rabbits, hares and pheasants at the Plough and Flail, in those days still nothing more than four terraced cottages.

Ernest Acton

At that time Mr Gillibrand rented the shooting rights to Saltersley Common to Mr Gass, the solicitor (father of Michael and Peter), but poaching was considered fair game. Everyone was at it. Reader relax, no one is going to name and shame!

Other roads leading directly on to the Moss include Gore Lane, which sounds rather bloodthirsty, but it appears as Gaw Lane on the eighteenth century tithe maps. Gaw is a British name of Celtic origin, meaning foreigner or stranger, and was often applied to settlers who arrived from Wales. Alternatively, it could derive from the old English *gara*, which means a triangular piece of land. Gaw could also come from the Welsh *gof*, which means a smith, so we must take our pick.

Upcast Lane is another very old route which skirted round the edges of the moss. The word 'upcast' derives from an old English word, *ceastal*, - a heap of stones. Although the name would seem to denote a mining connection, we have found no evidence of any such activity. The lane runs parallel with Knutsford Road up to Davenport Green and Lindow End. Behind what was, until recently, the site of the Cheshire Garage are the remains of a very ancient hedgerow.

Upcast was previously known as Filter Bed Lane. The filter beds were built in the 1800s and this was a land of sumps and soakaways - two of the soakaways were 60 feet deep. There was an engineer's shed, plus a bungalow that went with the job, for the pumping engineer, Billy Webb.

By the the 1950s constant water and sewage seepage had caused the grass to grow very high and this attracted a considerable number of corncrakes. They were always round the filter beds.

In 1963 Blaster Bates was hired to blow it all up, causing thunderous explosions which rocked the surrounding neighbourhood. The filtering operation was transferred to Noah's Ark Lane, Warford, on the opposite side of the Knutsford road, where the sewage farm and pumping station is still in action.

An old marker stone near the Knutsford Road bus shelter, just before the turning into Gravel Lane, leads us towards what was once extensive farmland which extended to Lindow End. This land belonged to Sunnybank Farm. It was owned at that time by John Pennington, who sold the fields for building in late 1948, when all the estates were built. Cumber Lane was originally a little country track called Whalley's Lane, after Andrew Whalley, listed as the tenant of Whalley's Farm in 1892.

CP

Row of Trees c1900, with the original huge lime trees, later felled as they had become diseased.
courtesy Wilmslow Library and Cheshire County Council

Row of Trees

Row of Trees House aka Smallwood House aka Plague Farm*

This very attractive timber-framed house stands opposite the actual row of trees, where the track from Chorley Old Hall near Alderley Edge crosses the Mobberley Road and goes on to German Joe's etc. It is T-shaped, a long house with a single cross-wing. 1585 in the Deeds. Against the cross wing is a big stone chimney stack with the following inscription:

EDMVND DUNCALFE

A:DNI 1607

From the garden side it can be seen that there is a tiny window in the side of this stack upstairs. There is a very big central stack too, sprouting from middle of the stone flag roof. This one is of brick with four diagonally set chimneys.

We enter by the kitchen door at the end, but to understand the house you need to start at the front door. Already a sharp eye will have noticed that the door and the big central chimney are apparently in line. Sure enough, it is a Baffle entry, a standard Cheshire type, where the door leads straight in to the side of the great fireplace, like Hanson House*. You are baffled, and have to turn either right or left. It is a good draught-excluding plan. The great inglenook beams seem to indicate that there was once a huge smoke hood here.

*See 'The March of Progress?' chapter.

The end chimney is a fine stone piece inside as well. In the upper room is a tiny room within the stack and lit by the little window we saw outside. The sale brochure has this as 'a priest hole'. It is not. It is a toilet. The groove for the seat is still there and, whizzing downstairs and outside to check, so is the digging-out hole at the bottom. An inside toilet or garderobe would have been a considerable status symbol in 1607, especially a heated one. I have seen another like it though. At Soss Moss Hall which is not far away the huge end stack which is signed and dated T. Wyche 1583 has no fewer that three toilets within it - two upstairs (his 'n' hers?) and one downstairs.

*For Plague stone E S 1665 story see Quaker chapter.

MH

Row of Trees House, front view

Row of Trees House, rear view

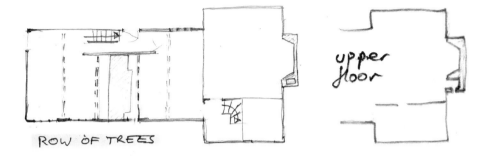

ROW OF TREES

upper floor

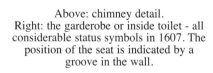

Above: chimney detail.
Right: the garderobe or inside toilet - all considerable status symbols in 1607. The position of the seat is indicated by a groove in the wall.

Behind the Row of Trees lives Mrs Rene Eckert, widow of Josef, aka German Joe, a well know local character who died only recently. "I'm German Joe" he used to introduce himself, with an outstretched hand and wide grin. Josef was born in Heidelberg in 1924, and volunteered to join the U-boat service in 1943 and after training was assigned as helmsman to a Type VII U-boat, code named U616. He served nine tours of duty, which was way beyond the odds of survival, steering U616 through the waters of the Atlantic, Iceland and Greenland.

By 1944 they had arrived in the Mediterranean and the U616 was depth charged by two US destroyers and HMS Haydock. The submarine was badly damaged but managed to reach the naval base at La Spezia, where it underwent extensive repairs and went on to sink four Italian submarines, following Italy's withdrawal from the Axis powers, plus several merchant ships.

Josef also participated in the longest U-boat chase in history during which they crossed the western Mediterranean from Ibiza to Oran, pursued for over 36 hours by a flotilla of US destroyers, together with the RAF's 36 Squadron of Wellington bombers. The U616 was finally scuttled on 17 May 1944 and the entire crew taken prisoner by the USS Ellyson. Lucky to survive, Josef spent the rest of the Second World War as a prisoner of the Americans, picking cotton in Mississippi. In May 1945

Rene Dann c1946 in The Yews doorway. In those days the coal man dropped off the coal in a pile at top of lane, near Studholme Kennels and they had to fetch it to the cottage in an old pram.
courtesy Rene Eckert

he was not repatriated, but transferred to Britain to endure a further two years of forced labour. He was sent to the Prisoner of War camp at Mobberley, where he was given farm work. He also met Rene Dann and following his release chose to remain in Mobberley. The couple married in 1948.

Rene and Josef Eckert were to spend all their married life at The Yews, way down at the bottom of a rough track which runs off the top end of Moor Lane. In earlier times the track was known as Clay Lane and may once have been an extension of the aforementioned Clay Lane, which leads from Moss Lane in Mobberley to Paddock Hill. The two Clay Lanes are only separated for a short distance by field paths.

The Yews is built on sand and the area in front of house is peat bog. The original small cottage was the family home of the Dann family, who came from Handforth. With four bedrooms and $2\frac{1}{2}$ acres of land, it was quite large compared to most of the moss cottages. Rene remembers back to her childhood years at The Yews, when the coalman refused to deliver to the door and used to tip the coal in a pile at the Moor Lane end of the track. It was the girls' task had to take an old pram and a shovel and make several journeys, trundling the latest delivery of coal back to the cottage.

Joe gradually enlarged the cottage, bought more land and spent the rest of his days farming beef cattle. The Yews now extends to 20 acres, much of which runs down towards the Row of Trees and Upcast Lane. Josef never forgot his wartime experiences and stayed in regular contact with all the surviving members of the U-616 until the end of his life.

CP

The painting of the U-616

Mrs Eckert with the
painting of the
U-616, to which Josef
was assigned helmsman
in 1943.

Josef, still a prisoner of war in 1946, was made to work as a farm labourer.
Seen here, aged 23, at Barber's Farm, Mobberley, with a shire horse.

courtesy Rene Eckert

The Croft

The Croft, on Newton Hall Lane has been in the Davies family for several generations. Until fairly recently it was a large holding encompassing several acres and various small enterprises. These included the Brick Field, which was used for brick making, the Croft Garage, latterly run by Denis Newton, the Croft Caravan site, the Croft Cafe, Croft Cottage c1800, Rose Cottage 1870, Graveyard Lane and Graveyard Farm. Also a tiny cottage - The Cottage on the little pathway leading to Moss Lane, which was tenanted by Vera Worsley for many years.

The original tenants of the Croft were Cyril Richardson and his wife, who started all the enterprises. Croft Garage began life as a shop and then two hand petrol pumps were installed. The caravan site was originally an overnight stop for towed caravans and was used by holiday makers en route to the coastal resorts of North Wales. It is now a large static site with around 30 mobile homes, each connected to mains services, with their own small area of garden. There are many long term residents, including one who has been there for 35 years and another for 30 years.

Croft Cafe was originally a shippon. There were two hatches in the wall through which drinks were served and the place proved very popular with American soldiers during war. Soon the enterprise was expanded to lay on entertainments, with music and dancing at the rear. It also became a venue for wedding receptions. Following the death of Cyril Richardson his widow absented herself down south and the Davies family tried to recover the tenancy. The court ordered them to pay Mrs Richardson out, despite her non residence. The joys of renting out property!

After his father died, John Davies and his family moved into the Croft, to be close to his mother who lived next door, at Rose Cottage. On the land surrounding Croft Cottage he has established a large collection of exotic species trees from all over the world.

Nothing here has rolled for many a year and the whole of the Croft is covered in moss; not just the land but the corrugated tin rooves of the old garage sheds, the surrounding stones - anything, in fact that has been left lying, as if the moss is struggling to reassert and reclaim something of its former self. But after many years the Croft Garage has just been vacated and I expect that, in the longer term, the moss will be fighting a losing battle.

CP

Croft Caravan Park 2002

Croft Garage, closed down and abandoned, September 2002

Graveyard Farm

Graveyard Farm was let to Samuel Jackson, formerly a tenant of Hollingee, who remained at the Graveyard until his death, upon which a complex court case ensued to cancel the Jackson tenancy and remove Samuel's daughter, Marion, who was trying to claim ongoing tenancy rights. By this time the property was in a poor state of neglect. Part of the Graveyard land was sold off to the constructors of Mobberley Golf Course and the farm itself, together with the burial ground, access lane and the remaining land and outbuildings was purchased by Stockport undertakers Bill and Margaret Arnison, who now offer green burials on a site adjacent to the old Quaker burial ground. Sadly, Bill died very suddenly shortly after we had interviewed him.

Graveyard Lane leads through to Moss Lane. Seventy years ago Ralph Hatton, of Lea Farm on Moss Lane, was paid to cut the grass in the burial ground. One dark night, after a night out, a young girl decided to take a shortcut home. This involved walking past the graveyard. It was late and she approached the burial ground with some trepidation. Suddenly chains began to rattle. Heart in mouth, she ran through to Moss Lane in absolute terror, thinking it was 'the spooks'. It was not until the following day that she discovered that Ralph had tethered two goats to graze the graveyard grass, to save himself the trouble!

Many of the old Quaker gravestones are missing, reputed to have been lifted, reversed and used to flag the kitchen floor at some nearby dwelling. This was not Graveyard Farm, as the late Bill Arnison assured me - he had lifted and checked all the flags during the course of his recent sensitive and loving restoration of Graveyard Farm.

A Green burial in progress when we visited, that of a Professor of Music attached to Manchester University. Designed for further occupancy, the grave had been dug to a depth of eight feet by hand and the grave diggers were waiting in the yard to fill it in after the short committal service by Margaret Arnison*

*See The Slough of Despond chapter.

Bill was a builder who had trained as an architect and it was obvious that he loved every minute of his time at Graveyard Farm. He restored the wreck of Graveyard Farm with care and sensitivity, taking huge pride in his work. The finished buildings now stand as a great credit and tribute to him. Two fields have been set aside for green burials, alongside the old Quaker graveyard and his wife Margaret and one of their sons are continuing to follow Bill's vision. Wildlife is encouraged and there are lambs in the field at the back of the farmhouse.

The tiny cottage where Vera Worsley lived has also been sold and is now greatly enlarged and almost unrecognisable. The pathway leads us down into Moss Lane, which skirts the southern edges of Lindow Moss. Moss Lane is very pretty and contains some highly desirable properties. Tucked amongst several barn conversions, and some more recently built houses, are the original moss cottages which have been extended and modernised beyond recognition. From the top end, which leads to Coppock House Farm, the long moss rooms are clearly visible, leading across towards Paddock Hill. Only Lea Cottage, next door to Lea Farm, has remained virtually unchanged both inside and out, and still retains its original windows. Down at the Knutsford Road end a tiny wooden bungalow - Pluto - stands alone, surrounded by fields, now a little wooden holiday house, similar to the sort of shack that formed the nucleus of many of the desirable homes of today.

CP

Date stone discovered in the cellars during the restoration of Graveyard Farm.

Moss Lane c1900

courtesy Jenny Nixon

Back of Graveyard Farm prior to restoration

courtesy Margaret and Bill Arnison

Behind German Joe's this old moss cottage remains unchanged since it was first built. Most of the properties around the edges of the moss would originally have looked very similar to this.

Large moss room extending from Paddock Hill through towards the Row of Trees, behind German Joe's.

Row of Trees (aka Plague House) Farm yard.

Pluto is a tiny wooden bungalow which stands alone, surrounded by fields, on Moss Lane.
Probably named after the pipeline, rather than the Disney character, it is now used as a holiday let.

HERE LYETH THE
BODY OF JOHN
KEY OF CARRIN
HALE WHO DYED
THE 22 DAY OF
THE 4 MONTH
1689

8
The Slough of Despond
Lindow In The 17th Century

The Slough of Despond
Lindow In The 17th Century

"... they drew nigh unto a very miry slough, that was in the midst of the plain; and they, being heedless did both fall suddenly into the bog. The name of the Slough was Despond. Here, therefore, they wallowed for a time, being grievously bedaubed with dirt; and Christian, because of the burden that was on his back, began to sink in the mire." John Bunyan

Pilgrim's Progress was written in jail. John Bunyan, tinker, Puritan, started his itinerant preaching in about 1654, walking the byways of England. He will have seen places like Lindow in their primitive state. He probably had to cross them, and will have talked to the people who lived there. Like many puritans he did not mince his words, using the experiences of his wanderings in his imagery of the Christian journey.

"This miry slough is such a place as cannot be mended; it is the descent whither the scum and filth that attend conviction for sin doth continually run, and therefore it is called the Slough of Despond. .... and this is the reason for the badness of this ground."

The Quakers

On the quiet byway between Moss Lane and Newton Hall Lane it is surprising to find, all by itself, a little graveyard. Just a grassy plot with a low wall round it and a few old gravestones. No chapel or church, no cross, not even a notice to tell us what it is. The extreme simplicity of the place is unusual, and the few stones are the same - no flowery epitaphs here or trumpeting angels.

This is the final resting place for some of the earliest of those people who called themselves Friends, and who were called Quakers. A peaceful resting place for bolshie people.

George Fox is credited as the founder of the Society of Friends, although it sprang out of the religious and social ferment of the times. 'Quakers' was a nickname given them by a judge in 1650 who was bidden by Fox to "tremble at the word of the Lord". The judge clapped him in jail, like Bunyan. The fledgling group was given some much-needed stability by the conversion in 1652 of Margaret Fell, of Swarthmoor near Ulverston. She turned her home into a refuge and powerhouse of the new movement.

The early Quakers were not quiet. That came later. They were

Early Quaker gravestone, burial ground, Mobberley

militant puritans who loudly condemned the wrongs and injustices of the world, urging common people to listen to the spirit within them and not to bow to the authority of church, state or wealth.

Soon after 1652, which is about as early as it can get, a group of religious dissidents came together in Morley for Meetings. The Quaker community in the area is still called Morley Meeting. They were persecuted. In 1665 the Churchwarden's Accounts of Wilmslow Parish Church report:

"1656 Distributed by Mr Brereton parson and the churchwardens XXs which was forfeited by the Quakers for their Saboth breaking and ordered for the poore of Wilmslow p'ish."

In 1665 a Meeting at a house in Mobberley was broken up by Captain Edwarde Alcocke, head constable, with the arrest of eighteen worshippers. Friends who visited them in jail were arrested too. The churchwardens' accounts continue:

1675	Spent when we sued (pursued?) the Quakers -	1/6
1675	Spent for serving execution upon the Quakers -	2/4
	Spent when we went to straine (distrain) the Quakers -	1/8
1676	Spent when we went about the brief for Northampton and selling the Quakers goods -	2/-

No wonder they met in such secluded surroundings. One meeting place was Yarwood House, the home of Richard Yarwood who was a founder member. Now cut off by Runway 2 from Lindow and Morley, it is a pretty brick small farm, dollified today but not painfully so, with two uneven gables and an off-centre entrance. Mike and Lucy Thomas live there today. It is the only building we have seen with a Cruck frame,

Interior, Yarwood House, showing the cruck.

Peace and tranquillity in a corner of the Quaker Burial Ground at Mobberley

"A handsome Meeting House was built, still a landmark .... with its well-proportioned red brick facade and big arched windows."

which is visible inside.

Another early meeting place was Hollingee. Open air meetings were held at the Row of Trees, a sort of no man's land equidistant from Wilmslow, Mobberley and Alderley churches.

The Graveyard was first used in 1656. It was just a corner of a field, perhaps rented. It was purchased in 1669 for £3, and extended a little in 1673. The earliest gravestone recorded is 1680. There were 400 burials here between 1650 and 1750. In the Mobberley church records we read: '1701 Mary Key, buryed at the Quakers Burying Ground, contrary to Act of Parl., for burying whereof was paid five pounds.'

In 1693 the Friends felt confident enough to build a little meeting house on the northern fringe of the bog. It is on a sharp bend (being straightened 2002) of the Altrincham Road. It was in use until 1830, when, an odd time span, the lease expired and the Friends had to find a new home. It was converted to 3 cottages. Now it is one house, called Penn House.

In 1831 the Friends acquired a new site - *'part of Lindow Common on the Edge of Wilmslow'*. It was used as a burial ground at first (1st burial 1832). A handsome Meeting House was built, still a landmark on the way into Wilmslow from the motorway with its well-proportioned red brick facade and big arched windows. In front can still be seen several of the very simple Quaker gravestones, often eschewing even the common names of the months - 'seventh month' for July - and certainly not running to decoration or to any expression of sentiment. The old graveyard on the Moss fell into disuse. The last burial there was in 1848. It was finally sold to Mr John Davies in 1977.

In 1883 a school had been built on top of the 1831 carriage shed next to the Meeting House. This was used for Adult Education too. The Wilmslow Guild had its origin here in 1926. Now the Guild has its own buildings, put up on part of the Quaker burying ground in 1963. It is still going strong, having celebrated its 75th Anniversary in 2001, and still independent.

In 1994, rather sadly (but Quakers are not sentimental about their buildings) the Morley Meeting moved out of its fine Meeting House, which was sold into business use, and into the converted school next door.

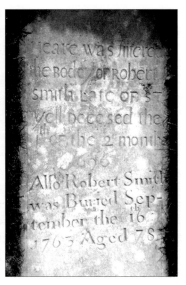

The Baptist Chapel at Great Warford

Warford is immediately south of Lindow Moss and the story of Warford Chapel parallels that of the Quakers. The story starts during the chaos of the Civil War when a group of parliamentary soldiers of Puritan persuasion met together in an unnamed farmhouse. Believing that only those who had been born again in the faith could be baptised, they were aligned with the Baptist church, was in the process of coalescing out of the ferment of the times. Adults were baptised, just as John baptised converts in the Jordan, in a handy river or spring. In this case the baptising place was said to have been near Chorley Old Hall, which is pretty close by. There is a good little spring between Chorley Hall and Row of Trees, near Common Carr Farm.

They soon moved to Pownall Brow Farm, near Lindow End. In 1712 the congregation felt confident enough to convert a cottage and barn into a permanent chapel, which is still in use today. But they must already have had use of the site because the earliest gravestone is 1671.

It is a diminutive building, brick on the front which presumably dates to 1712 but still timber-framed at the back. The steep pitch of the stone roof indicates that it was originally thatched. Round metal plates on the two doors, both with the mark and date NOTHE4 1712 scratched into them, are what is left of knockers like that still on the front door of Antrobus Hall of 1709, on Faulkner's Lane nearby. The Antrobus family were strong supporters of the breakaway Brook Street chapel in Knutsford, so there may be a connection here.

The Painted Board At Mobberley Church

If the eighteenth century was the age of taste and gravitas, the nineteenth that of industry and empire, and the twentieth - well it is too soon to say, the seventeenth was a time of the utmost ferment. London was racked by plague and then consumed by fire. The King was executed outside his own Banqueting Hall. Rival armies fought up and down the land. The church, having broken away from Rome, was riven by dissent from within and without, and when priests who refused to conform were chucked out they refused to be quiet, preaching to rival congregations in the fields and barns. Women were persecuted as witches.

An echo of these extraordinary times can be got by looking at a memorial in Mobberley church. It is not carved stone nor painted glass, but a flat wooden board like an Inn sign. Indeed it was probably painted by a sign painter. It hangs high up on the chancel wall and is hard to see because of the shine off the black and gold paint.

It commemorates Elizabeth, wife of Nathaniel Robinson and daughter of Samuel Shipton, who died in 1665. Nathaniel was the son of Robert Robinson whose initials RR 1620 are inscribed on a beam of Hill House*.

See 'The March of Progress?' chapter

Samuel Shipton, *'an honest learned gentleman'*, was the Rector of Alderley. He was booted out of his post in 1643 by the puritans, because he was a Royalist. When Charles II recovered the throne in 1660 he managed to get his job back, but was magnanimous to the interloper, Nicholas Stevenson, finding him a living in Chester.

Nathaniel and Elizabeth had only been married for two years when she died.

The memorial is a complete C17 sermon on death, a subject that must have been on everyone's mind in that fateful year. The dog latin and the mixture of Christian doctrine and classical allusion suggest that Sam Shipton is the author.

The winged cupid at the top invites the soul to rest from its labours and be at peace in 'Elysium'. Below the clouds the delightfully rustic trumpeting angels, cousins to those in the Booths' town house in Knutsford (see 'A Window on Knutsford' p. 45), greet the ascending soul who is shown as a winged and feathered eye - surely an Egyptian motif. The corpse is shown but we are told *'this diseased husk cannot pass over'*. Below that is Elizabeth's epitaph. She died in the winter solstice but in the springtide of her years. *'Reader, do not seek for her ashes here'* - so she must be buried elsewhere.

My thanks to Shelagh Proctor for translating the text.

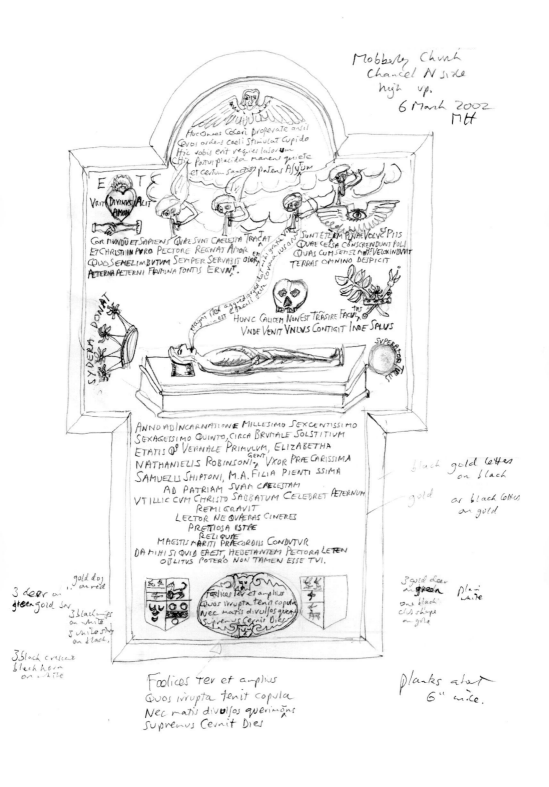

Foelices ter et amplius
Quos irrupta tenit copula
Nec malis divulsos querimons
supremus Cernit Dies

Planks about 6" wide.

The Plague Story 1665

On the 16th of July 1665 a woman came fleeing into Cheshire, to cast herself on the mercy of her relations at Row of Trees Farm. She was a refugee from London, where the Great Plague was raging.

It had started sometime in 1664, carried, we now know, by shipboard rats. In the early stages thousands fled the city, but by the summer of 1665 the remaining citizens were virtually prisoners in their houses, barred from leaving by emergency edicts and anyway with nowhere to flee to since no one would take them in.

How she escaped we do not know. We do know that her relations refused to take her in, putting her instead in the barn on the corner of Carr Lane. They apparently fed her off a pikel (pitchfork, hence pikelets). But she died anyway.

'E. Staneaw, buried at her own house 17 July 1665, she being suspected to dye of the plague, she but coming the day before.'

There is supposed to be a stone in the field bearing the initials E.S. 1665, where she was buried. We could not find it.

Green Funerals

Let us finish on a peaceful note, and return to the Quaker Graveyard on the Moss. It is a surprise to see new burials in an adjacent plot. They, like the Quaker burials, have a simplicity about them - no imported granites and marbles here. The sentiments too, while Quakers would never have expressed any sentiment at all, are unusual:

> *I believe in the sun even when it is not shining*
> *I believe in love even when I feel it not*
> *I believe in God even when he is silent.*

It turns out that this is a plot for Green Funerals. It was started by Bill and Margaret Arnison of Graveyard Farm. Free of overt religious symbolism, eco-friendly, very much in tune with our time. Although unconnected with the Quakers it seems to be fulfilling some of its principals.

Bill Arnison died suddenly in 2002, and was given a green funeral. His own grave, all by itself as yet, is at the bottom of the field, by the barn of Graveyard Farm.

MH

Bill Arnison at Graveyard Farm, May 2002

9
*Civilising The Bog
Dwellers*

Civilising The Bog Dwellers

Lindow Moss was a raucous, disreputable, uncontrolled sort of place, where people built themselves unauthorised shacks and then lived in them, where anyone could dig the peat for a fire, where children were left to play unsupervised and where the Gypsies roamed, setting up for the night on one of the green roads with their bow-topped van and letting the horse graze, unasked, a neighbouring field. No doubt there were widespread social problems. Poverty. Inebriation. Fights. Irregular family relationships. Illiteracy and ignorance. Dirt and ill-health. For all that though there was a freedom that many must have envied, and that was indeed made a romance of by 'Romany', alias the Rev George Bramwell Evans, whose van is parked up as a museum piece next to the public library in Wilmslow.

The Old Workhouse was built in 1773 on reclaimed bog land opposite Lindow Common, where Gorsey Bank school is now. The 'workus' was not aimed at improving bog dwellers. It had a wider remit of relieving the parish of caring for those who could not care for themselves. It was built at Lindow because a Workhouse was an undesirable neighbour, and Lindow was a suitable dumping ground. Its successor, the Union Workhouse in Knutsford, is proudly blazoned BUCKLOW 1897 in red terracotta. Like Lindow workhouse it was built in an undesirable spot, although you would not think so today. It was next to the grim Knutsford prison, which was demolished in the 1920s and eventually replaced by Booth's supermarket. Workhouses often turned into hospitals, as this one has.

Stanley Chapel was built by the Methodists at Lindow End in 1839. Now closed, it was so called because it was built on a minute parcel of land belonging to the Stanleys of Alderley Park, who had a few scattered moss room fields and cottages nearby. Their donation of the land to build the chapel is a little surprising in view of the family's antipathy to Methodism in a previous generation, when Methodists met in the kitchen at Soss Moss Hall.

The Stanleys also owned the land on which **Lindow School** was built in 1858, next to the Row of Trees but separated from it by a terrace of cottages. Paid for by John Heugh, a wealthy Manchester merchant and shipper, who had built himself a grand Italianate villa, Firwood, at Alderley Edge, it is now a Kingdom Hall belonging to the Jehovah's Witnesses.

The Victorian age was a great one for self-improvement, and for the

Opposite: St John's Church, Lindow

The Old Workhouse Altrincham Road, demolished in 1939.

courtesy Stella Willett

Lindow School, built near the Row of Trees in 1858, now a Kingdom Hall belonging to the Jehovah's Witnesses.

improvement of others. Those who made their fortunes in Manchester - and there were fortunes to be made - built themselves villas in nice places like Wilmslow and Alderley Edge, where the air was clean. Their consciences - another Victorian speciality - often dictated that they should exercise philanthropy in the city that their money came from. Take James Jardine of 'Brookdale', on Brook Lane Alderley Edge. He had climbed up by his own bootstraps to be the head of a major cotton empire, but he never forgot where he had come from, supporting and endowing Ancoats hospital, Owens College, and the Cathedral.

In their new country homes the incomers were perhaps surprised to find that the lot of some of the natives was little better than that of the workers back in the smoky city.

Morley Chapel at Morley Green, a relict piece of common land on the fringe of the bog, is a sweet building, of striped brickwork under a comfortable catslide roof. It would be good to identify the architect. I would like to think he was JW Beaumont, who also designed St John's church on the other side of Lindow.

It was founded by Robert Crewdson, a Manchester Industrialist and neighbour of James Jardine at Alderley Edge. He asked James White of the Manchester City Mission to start an evangelical mission at Morley in 1862. A cottage was hired for congregational worship, and classes were held in Religious education for the local children.

Before long the people felt the need for a place of their own. A building fund was started. Land had to be found. Nobody owned any, but David Henshall was able to prove squatters' rights over Sir Humphrey de Trafford, and so sold his patch for £120. The chapel was opened on 21st February 1869. The first superintendent was Joseph Wood. The day school was started in 1874 under Mrs Scott. By 1900 it was a mixed school for 100 children under Miss Ashbrook and Miss Alcott.

Joseph Wood died in 1900. His successor was his son-in-law John Beaumont (pronounced Bewmont by Eric Worsley), who when he died in 1925 had served the chapel for fifty-seven years. Four arty stained glass windows by Walter J Pearce are his memorial. Morley Chapel has its own First World War Memorial, to the nine Morley men who were killed, including John Acton, George Bradley and Fred Potts. A beautiful mosaic plaque, designed and made again by Walter J Pearce, who lived locally.

Since 1972 it is Morley United Reformed Church. It is no longer a school but Morley Chapel continues its mission and service to the local people. A world away from the Cheshire Smokehouse next door.

The Morley Club is another example of cottontot philanthropy. Harold Agnew came to live at Stamford Lodge, on the Altrincham Road, in 1916. The Agnews were prominent Manchester Liberals, art dealers to the

Morley Chapel at Morley Green, opened on 21st February 1869.

newly rich, and owners of 'Punch'. It was through his wife's influence that a social club came to be established, first of all in the Chapel. Soon the burgeoning membership felt the need of a clubhouse of their own, but the usual problems arose, viz. a) no money, b) no land. Problems are meant for solving. Sir Humphrey de Trafford was persuaded to donate a piece of land opposite the chapel, and at the end of the Great War army huts were available. A hut brought from Kinmel camp in North Wales was the club's first home. It was opened by Mrs Shimwell, another cottontot from Alderley Edge. Kinmel huts were recycled all over the place as clubhouses, scout huts, temporary classrooms and dwellings. Many still stand, but the Morley one was rebuilt in 1930.

Lindow St John's Church is on the urban fringe of the bog, where Lindow meets Wilmslow. It is built in Church-of-England gothic but is modest in its ambition, with a simple big roof and no tower. St John's was founded by Rev James Whitworth Consterdine, first vicar of St Philip's Alderley Edge. For some years services had been held in Lindow School, but in 1872 the decision was made to build a proper church. £2,400 pounds was collected and subscribed - not a huge sum even in those days. An architect, J W Beaumont, and a builder B Heywood, both local men, were appointed and the foundation stone was laid on 21st June 1873. It didn't take long to build; the first service in the completed building was on the 16th January 1875. The first priest was WS Barnes, or Barnes-Slacke. The second vicar was R H Consterdine, the founder's own son, who served St John's from 1904 until his death in 1938. A big Vicarage was built for him in 1908, which unlike many old vicarages is still is use as such. In 1915 he built a Parish Room, quite a striking building with two octagonal towers in front. The Cricket Club opposite was established in 1924 on land given by Esther Barnes, sister of the first vicar. Today Lindow church is a very popular and youthful one.

The urge to tidy up Lindow and civilise the bog dwellers has had many other manifestations. Doing away with the gipsy racetrack, and making the Common into a proper park. Building a proper pub, the Boddington Arms, instead of the highly irregular Long Bar. Capping the wells that all the bog houses had, and laying on mains water. And, I think, building them little white houses. A great many of the bog houses have a single-roomed extension, properly built of white-painted brick with a slate roof. It would seem that these were added to shacks of one sort or another, often of wood, to provide at least one bit of decent accommodation. Nowadays the shacks are nearly all rebuilt into nice bungalows, but the white extensions are still there and visible.

MH

10
The Last Bog
Dwellers
Left Alive

The Last Bog Dwellers Left Alive

Most people seem to have ended up living on the bog due to misfortune of one sort or another. Dispossessed, homeless, poverty stricken or outcast due to some fall from social grace.

During the 1920s Stormy Point, at the junctions of Moor Lane, Cumber Lane and Battery Lane (now Rotherwood Road), was still a fairly self contained little community. A few small shops stocked the basic necessities and were a life line for the bog dwellers, marooned on the outskirts of the town without transport or means of communication. Jas Robson had his bike shop there, and also sold or re-charged radio batteries for the local populace. Once a week fish could be bought from one of the cottages. The fish was left on trust in a bucket of ice inside the porch and customers took their pick, wrapped it in newspaper provided and left their money in a dish on the shelf. James's ran the newsagents, and there was a choice of two small, old fashioned grocers' shops - Browns and Cunliffes. Platts, the drapers, supplied household and personal items. Mr Hart travelled around by cart, selling haberdashery and housewares. He also supplied paraffin and fire lighters. Later he abandoned the horse and cart and upgraded to a Morris three ton truck.

Mr Bill Whittaker, who now lives in a neat cottage on Park Road remembers his childhood days living on the bog in the early 1920s. Aged 81, he is the oldest of the bog dwellers that we managed to track down. His mother was widowed with three children, who were Bill's half sisters and brother.

"My brother was seven when I was born. He always looked after me and took me to school. We had to walk all the way to Nursery Lane and back - about four miles each way. The only place she could find for us was a wooden shack with a tin roof on the bog - on the sandy part at the back there - turned into two rooms by a flimsy partition. There was a chimney and an old black range. We collected wood and dug turf for cooking. There was no gas or electricity. We fetched water from a spring - it was a good spring.

Black Tom lived in a big tent behind us and kept goats. We bought our milk off him. I think he was a Russian. Other families I remember were the Frosts, the Ellams and the James's. Eddie Bailey ran the turf-cutters, the bog site and the shacks - he rented them out to desperate families.

We played on the bog and lit some fires, but it was just lads' mischief in those days - nothing like the awful criminal stuff you hear about kids getting up to nowadays. I remember the 1920s King's Cup Air Race. I'd never seen a plane till then. It flew over the bog and the pilot

Opposite: Ernest Burgess 1876-1948, at Wilmslow Gas Works, where he worked on retorts.
courtesy Jim and Fred Burgess

128

waved to us! We could see him quite clearly. After my grandmother died we moved to her old cottage in Chapel Lane - its where the Green Room Theatre is now."

The story of how the Burgess family came to live on the bog is a sad one. Originally they had lived in one of two small cottages on Green Lane, near to the Catholic Church. When a new priest arrived it was decided to provide him with better accommodation, so the tenants were turned out and the cottages demolished to make way for the smart new presbytery. With no compensation and nowhere to turn, the desperate Mrs Burgess found one third of a shack to rent on the bog.

Born into a Catholic family of five boys and two girls, the Burgess brothers are the last living members. Although Jim and Fred remain Catholics, their mother never set foot inside a Catholic Church again. Jim was born in 1925 and Fred in 1928, making them a few years younger than Bill Whittaker, who had already moved from the bog before the Burgess family arrived.

Fred was conceived and born in the bog shack, again rented from Eddie Bailey. Two other families, the James and the Ellams shared this shack with them. It was a long wooden building with a tin roof, not on stilts but built directly onto the ground,, rather like a long stable to accommodate six horses. To this long wooden shelter had been added three chimney flue outlets, one for each of the black cooking ranges. There was a *"bit of a garden"* surrounding it.

Each family unit was partitioned into two to create one living area and one bedroom. This was where Mr and Mrs Burgess and their seven children managed to make a home for themselves. There were five families, all in dire straights, living in this little settlement in the sand hills of the bog. The others were the Frosts, who lived in a separate shack to the rear, and the Munnerleys who lived on a small woodland enclosure a short distance away, on the opposite side of the track.

The Burgess family lived on the bog from 1928 - Fred was born in the September - until 1931 when they moved to South Oak Lane. They remember Joby Moor, a strange loner from Morley who lived on the tip at Newgate and built himself a crude shelter from rubbish he appropriated - or rather misappropriated - from the tip. He also kept goats.

Despite all their little differences - understandable under the circumstances -the five families seem to have developed a collective bonding. They were outsiders - beyond the pale. Despised and stigmatised, they all rallied together at any sign of trouble. A 'strength in numbers' mentality to survive. The children walked barefoot to school, pushing an old pram, which contained their boots. These they put on before entering the school gates. Once a week, after school they pushed the empty pram to the Gas Works down Church Street and filled it with coke. They then pushed it back home, where it was mixed with the peat turves so that it burnt hotter for the cooking.

Every year the men cut down the encroaching bracken and burnt it on a bonfire. Aged two, little Fred kicked his football towards the bonfire. Running to save the precious ball he fell into the flames. He was wearing short trousers and wellingtons, which saved his legs, but his knees, hands, arms and face were terribly burnt. Mr Ellam pulled him out. There was no handy telephone for emergencies and no means of transport, so no medical attention was available. Fred's distraught mother dressed the burns with olive oil, which was quite the wrong thing to do. The following day a doctor did came out and gave him painkillers, but there was no hospital, no skin grafts. Fred stammered very badly for many years afterwards and still bears the scars.

It wasn't all bad. In the summer holidays and after school the bog children went off in a group to go swimming in the Bollin.

"We went for the day - took a picnic and bottles of pop. We used to push the pram there, with an old wind-up gramophone. We walked past Saltersley Hall to Burleyhurst Bridge, then down Eccups Lane to Morley Green Road. Opposite Oak Farm we turned up Dooleys Lane and crossed the Bollin at Tay Bridge or Oversley Ford. That's were little Fred learnt to swim - we just kept chucking him in the water! A lovely deep pool at a big bend in the river."

Fred worked at Cleggs Department Store on the corner of Hawthorn Lane and Bank Square and he used to be Santa Claus in the run up to Christmas. Jim and Fred now live together in the small terraced cottage to which their family finally moved in 1931.

CP

Fred and Jim Burgess, 2002

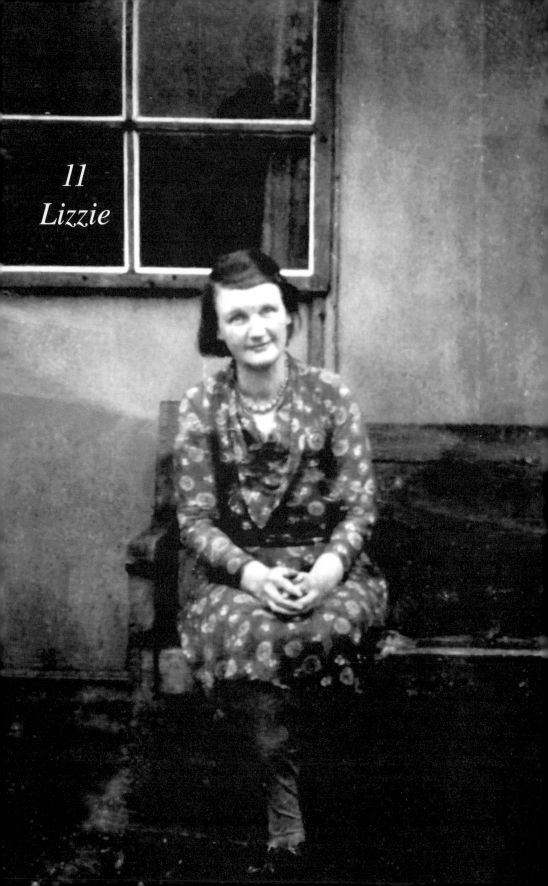

11
Lizzie

Lizzie

Amongst this raggle taggle of poor striving families and their numerous children, one woman struggled alone. On a small 'island' of land on the opposite side of the track from the rest of the bog families lived Elizabeth Munnerley. Everyone knew Lizzie. No account of the Lindow bog dwellers would be complete without her story. It is recounted here with the consent of her son, Walter, and Sue Dyer, probably the favourite of her many grandchildren. I have to thank them both for their frankness and cooperation. Time heals, and from this distance pattern of her life can be seen in its true perspective. She coped with dreadful vicissitudes with a tough survivor's instinct which one can only admire. In her own way Lizzie was both stoic and courageous.

Born in Lancashire in 1900, Elizabeth Munnerley was destined to be one of life's unfortunates. She was one of a number of children born to a woman who 'married' a few times, and had left numerous children scattered around the north west - some in Burnley, some in Colne. The same pattern was to be repeated years later, when Lizzie and her children, together with her disabled brother Jerry, were left abandoned on the bog.

At the age of six, Lizzie started work as a bobbin girl at a cotton mill in Colne, where small children were employed to run between the machinery collecting the empty bobbins. Here Lizzie witnessed numerous accidents. Many of the young children suffered injury; some were maimed and some lost their lives. There was no formal schooling for Lizzie, but she did learn to read and write, probably in the classroom set up at the mill for the child labourers. She eventually went on to become a weaver.

To say that her home background was bad is understating the case. Small boned and less than 5 feet tall, throughout her childhood Lizzie had been repeatedly abused by a series of common law 'step fathers'.

Lizzie's mother moved to the Wilmslow area c1922, bringing with her some of her brood, including Lizzie and her sibling Jerry, who was two years younger. Mr Ashton, who had money, finally made Mama respectable, but by that time the damage had been done. The remaining children went with her and their new stepfather to America, where some descendants still remain. Walter occasionally receives e-mail from transatlantic Munnerleys who are trying to research their family tree! Mr and Mrs Ashton eventually ended up in the Isle of Man and when she died Mrs Ashton left everything to her sister, Louisa Maud Munnerley.

Opposite: Elizabeth Munnerley at Woodside View c1929   *courtesy Walter Munnerley*

Lizzie's mother, a photograph taken after
she became Mrs Ashton.
courtesy Walter Munnerley

The Homestead, an ex-army hut purchased from Kinmel Camp, became home to the Ashton family until
they departed for America, leaving Lizzie and Jerry behind at Woodside View, a smaller Kinmel hut.
courtesy Walter Munnerley

Andrew Hulme, Great Grandfather of Cyril Bradley*, at the door of Mossways Farm, now demolished.
*See 'Peat' chapter.
courtesy Cyril Bradley

Walter and Alice Hulme of Mossways Farm. Alice was the daughter of James Morton, the *"miserly old hermit who had obtained the land by dint of squatter's rights"*, which he later sold to the Ashtons, including the parcel where Lizzie was to spend most of her life.
courtesy Cyril Bradley

First World War postcards from Kinmel Park, showing the layout of the camp and an interior view of one of the huts.
The postcard containing the verse is dated 5 March 1918.

By 1924 Lizzie, apparently unaware that she was pregnant, had given birth to a daughter, Louisa Maud, whose birth was never registered. The father, a local man, never acknowledged his illegitimate daughter.

In 1928 Mr Ashton appears to have funded the purchase of two parcels of land from James Morton, a miserly old hermit who had obtained the land by dint of squatter's rights. Originally from Morley, Jimmy Morton was the great-great grandfather of Cyril Bradley, who many years later acquired the peat-cutting rights at Saltersley.

Jimmy lived in some sort of hut and spent most of his time hunched over a bog fire, which he kept going all the time. Cyril's grandfather was Walter Hulme, who married James Morton's daughter, Alice. Cyril spent a great deal of his childhood at his grandparents' home at Moss Ways Farm, Eccups Lane - now demolished to make way for the static caravan site. Later in life Jimmy had linked up with some lady in the Potteries, and had coal mining connections. Cyril Bradley remembers him as *"gaunt, thin and old. Sat by his fire all rucked up. Alice and Uncle Arthur, who lived at Oldham and worked in the cotton mills, were his children. Alice used to take her father food in a basket."*

Notwithstanding this mean and miserable lifestyle, James Morton lived into his eighties and died in 1934. He is buried in a pauper's grave in Mobberley churchyard, in the middle of the triangle of pathways.

Great Grandad Hulme left the farm to his son Walter for his lifetime only - he lived there like a tenant. After Walter died it passed to his brother Alan, who sold it. Mossways Farm was built c1700 and had been in the Hulme family for generations.

The largest piece of land purchased by Mr Ashton was at the Saltersley end of Newgate, where The Homestead still stands. Both Woodside View and The Homestead were First World War ex-army huts, purchased from Kinmel Camp in North Wales. The Homestead is much larger than the hut which was bought to house Lizzie, and had probably served originally as a hospital ward for convalescent soldiers. The Homestead is now used by the Humane Society.

The second parcel of land, where Lizzie lived, was purchased for £100 and became the site of Woodside View. It appears to have been bought with the intention of providing somewhere out of the way for Lizzie, her brother Jerry and her daughter Louisa to live when the rest of the new family of Ashtons left for the United States. Abandoned on the bog, Lizzie and Jerry did not get on. Born a cripple in 1902, Jerry was another of life's losers. *"She was an outcast, left behind on the bog. Uncle John may have visited once."*

Lizzic's hut had a stove with an iron pipe for a chimney and asbestos to stop the wood catching fire. There was a corrugated iron roof and a chemical toilet. Without gas and electricity, they managed with oil lamps and candles. Water was carried from a well spring in the sand hills.

Lizzie's son, Walter, was born in Cranford Lodge in either 1931 or 1932. Even Walter doesn't know for sure, for once again Lizzie never registered the birth. He has had endless difficulties in proving his existence to the various authorities and has still never managed to get a passport. When he retired the State Pensions department eventually settled for 1932 as the official date, possibly depriving him of a year's pension rights.

As soon as she was able, Lizzie returned to her work as a weaver at Gregg's mill. Setting off at dawn, she walked there and back every day, winter and summer, as she was to do for the rest of her working life. Louisa walked to Fulshaw school, on Nursery Lane, where the Burgess brothers were her classmates and young Walter was left with Mrs Ryder* in the veteran Gypsy caravan and the old lady looked after him whilst his mother went to her work at Styal Mill. Walter remembers the Gypsy van as *"huge and very dark inside, with just one tiny window in the back. You had to climb up a steep flight of wide wooden steps to get inside. Old Mrs Ryder was all right and I liked it in there."*
*See 'Bog Dwellers Not Forgotten' chapter.

In 1937/38 Lizzie was in hospital at Macclesfield, where she gave birth to twins. Just prior to the birth Walter and his half sister were taken into care and placed into separate residential homes in Knutsford. Louisa went to the Racefield home for girls and Walter was at Kilrie, which has only recently been demolished. The twins, a boy and a girl, were named John and Betty. John died in the hospital within a week or so of his birth. Lizzie returned to Woodside View with the surviving twin and shortly afterwards journeyed to Knutsford to take Louisa and Walter back home. There was no transport available and Walter remembers them being escorted home in a police car.

The new baby did not thrive and Lizzie took her frequently to the clinic at Altrincham. Walter remembers pushing Betty around Newgate in the pram. After spending some time "isolated in a tent", the baby girl died at home. She was four or five months old. Louisa and Walter looked on as Lizzie took a compact mirror out of her bag and held it to Betty's lips to see if she was still breathing. There was a small, contained outbreak of diphtheria in the locality around this period and this may have been the cause of Betty's death. She is buried in a communal unmarked grave.

Once a week Walter and Lizzie collected coke from the gas works on Church Street in a pram - *"we'd ride it down, push it back"* - to mix with the peat. It was paid for at the gas showroom - *"a hut at the back, and they issued us with a ticket to collect our coke"*.

When he was old enough Walter used to go and help with 'dipping the turves'. This was done behind Eddie Bailey's cottage in Morley - just on the left as one turns into the lane to Morley Green. The peat was cut into squares and, after drying, dipped into a mixture of oil and paraffin before being sold house to house from a cart.

Walter always refers to his mother as 'the old lady'. He remained at Woodside View with Lizzie until his marriage to Mary in 1959. They have lived happily on Alma Lane ever since.

Following the outbreak of war Louisa worked in a munitions factory. One day she put her name and address inside a box of tools. It was picked out by a soldier, who came in search of her. Walter William Bennet found Louisa having a crafty smoke in the bottom of the tank which she was supposed to be cleaning. They were soon married and went on to produce 13 children!

The seventh of those children was Sue Dyer, verger of St Bartholomew's Church. Sue spent a lot of her childhood with Lizzie and has many happy memories of playing at Woodside View and around the peat bog. She and Lizzie seemed to have greatly enjoyed each other's company. *"I loved going to stay with my Gran. We had a lot of fun together. We were always laughing."* Lizzie, not uncommonly, seems to have derived more pleasure from her grandchildren than she did from her own. Sue remembers the exchange of peat for cakes. Some of the peat diggers gave her peat turves for Granny and they were used to fire up the old range. Cakes were baked, which they shared with the peat diggers!

By that time Jerry was having problems and was in and out of Parkside Hospital. Sue used to stay over and probably got to know Lizzie better than anyone. Later in life the old lady must have decided that the time had finally come when she was due a little respect. She hated being called Lizzie. *"My name is Elizabeth."* she would reprimand, sternly. It made little difference - Lizzie she was and Lizzie she remained.

She appears to have been quite strict with Sue, who was absolutely forbidden to go anywhere near Burleyhurst Bridge. This was probably because little Marie, the young daughter from Burleyhurst Farm, had fallen into the brook in the 1940s, grazing her arm. She died later of septicaemia.

Sue was allowed to play with the Gypsy children around Lizzie's place. There were about six of them and they used to put ropes in the trees and perform circus tricks.

"I had a tree house there, too. I often used to go back to their caravans in Eccups Lane and near Lindow Farm and they would invite me to stay and eat with them. My Gran always told me to thank them for having me and not to overstay my welcome. She wanted me to be polite."

Lizzie in the lovely woodland setting of Woodside View in the 1970s, pictured here with her grandson Phillip. Jerry's motor bike can be seen in the background.

courtesy Walter Munnerley

Lizzie aged 75, surrounded by members of her family, including thirteen grandchildren, following the marriage of Sue to Ernie Dyer.

courtesy Sue Dyer

This was in the 1960s, when the Gypsies still used to come to Lindow for the summer. By this time the vans were large and modern.

"I used to think they were like space ships - all silver and shining. And they had enormous old cars to tow them around. I was a bit of a tomboy in those days - always daring the lads. By that time I knew the peat bog like the back of my hand and I knew where was safe and where wasn't. I'd invented this game called Jumping the Ditches and I'd had a lot of practice. I was brilliant at it. One lad fell in trying to jump the big main ditch at the back of Woodside View and landed in the smelly water! Lizzie became interested in making a little garden and I helped her to plant it up. We put in all the different sorts of daffodils. We planted the two pink climbing roses in 1962."

The only roses on the entire peat bog, they still struggle into bloom each summer.

By this time the well spring in the sand hills had gone, probably due to changes in the water courses brought about by the continuous extraction of peat. Water was now fetched by Lizzie and Sue in two large containers from Boundary Farm on Eccups Lane, in the pram, which must have been extremely hard work, given the distances involved and the state of the track.

By the end of the 1960s Jerry had moved back to Partington, Lancashire. He had always had a passion for brass bands and one day he was out cycling and thought that he could hear a band in the distance. He set off down a country lane to try to find it and was hit by a car towing a caravan and killed outright. Lizzie, Louisa and Sue, then aged 16, travelled to the mortuary at Partington to identify the remains.

Although Lizzie had always fought with Jerry, as outcasts they were united and there must have been a strong bond between them. Lizzie was devastated by his death and never really got over it. Within a year she was taken to a warden controlled flat at Mallory Court, Mobberley.

"She resisted leaving Woodside View. When the health and safety people turned up she threatened to bash them over the head with a plank of wood! She was always very forthright, my Gran. Never afraid to speak her mind! It took her a long time to settle into Mallory Court. She found it strange, getting used to turning on taps and light switches. She really missed her little wooden place and her bit of land and the views, even though it was always a struggle."

Sue Dyer thinks that her grandmother had grown to despise men - small wonder - and when, at the age of twenty, Sue announced her engagement to Ernest Dyer, he was told in no uncertain terms that *"You'd better look after my granddaughter or I'll have you!"*.

Last of the joint inheritors, Walter still owns the piece of land. A demolition order was put on the poor shack and Walter pulled it down himself, after Lizzie had gone to Mallory Court. He is nervous about the peat extraction people digging it up. The approach lane, which is quite wide and wild, used to be an access track for the trucks to take away the peat. As a boy, Walter helped the drivers to lay bricks and rubble as hardcore, to prevent the laden vehicles getting bogged down.

Lizzie spent the last 13 years of her life at Mallory Court, with all mod cons. She died in 1984, as old as the century that fashioned her. Elizabeth Munnerley's direct descendants include 15 grandchildren, at least 30 great grandchildren and, to date, five great-great grandchildren

The current peat extraction is going around Lizzie's parcel of land and this reinforces the impression of standing on a small island. Undisturbed now for many years, it is a wonderful green oasis, private and secret, hidden away in the midst of a desert of peat. Lizzie is long gone, but the site of Woodside View has become a sanctuary for something else.

The badgers live there now and there are several entrances to their sett amongst the undergrowth. One wonders if they sleep away their days undisturbed by the noise and vibrations which must pass through their subterranean abode as the excavator hacks deep pits and trenches around the perimeters of the site.

A few artefacts poke up through the peaty soil. The spout from a huge copper kettle, turned green now, a broken piece of blue and white pottery from the wash stand, a well used old fashioned tin pie dish. Sad little remnants of bygone days. Times may have been hard and difficult and life unkind, but on a warm summer afternoon one could almost envy Lizzie her little patch. She loved it dearly.

CP

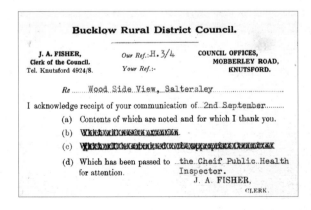

Lizzie's grandaughter Sue Dyer, verger of Bartholomew's Church, Wilmslow.

Mary and Walter Munnerley, now happily retired, enjoying the summertime in their garden.

The larger of the two Kinmel Park huts, The Homestead, still survives and is now the Newgate headquarters of the Humane Society, an animal sanctuary.

12
Peat

Peat

Peat is fossil fuel in the making. It consists of plant remains, full of fixed carbon, prevented from decay by the strange conditions of a peat bog: wetness, acidity, lack of oxygen, and cold. When dried out it makes a good fuel which glows rather than flames, making the characteristic smell which is still familiar in Ireland.

Lindow was a raised peat bog, with several distinct stages in its formation. There was once, maybe eight thousand years ago, a mere here, like Tabley Mere perhaps. Its margin would have been a good place to live, and it is possible that places like Saltersley and Row of Trees were inhabited even then. It slowly silted up and filled with reeds and fen, exactly as we can see happening today at the place called the Moor in the middle of Knutsford, where you feed the ducks. This process is being scientifically recorded as it happens, at Esthwaite in Cumbria. Towards the end of the Bronze Age trees grew out over the soggy fen, resulting in a very mysterious and impassable place, neither land nor water, full of fallen and rotting willows and stagnant pools. To see such a place we need only to return to Knutsford and peer down at Sanctuary Moor which lies between the Macclesfield and Toft Roads. Once the lake is completely filled up another process can begin. Sphagnum moss starts to grow on top. As it grows the place that was once a hollow becomes a low dome instead. The Sphagnum creates its own environment: acid, oxygen-free. The trees choke and die. Now we have a true peat bog, growing and spreading.

The raised bogs were at their most active phase of growth during the Celtic Iron Age. The bog land edge attracted marginal people, for peat is a poor man's fuel. When peat is cut the processes of the bog's formation are reversed and its history is revealed. First it has to be drained. Drainage ditches can be seen all over Lindow, usually flowing with tea-coloured peaty water but occasionally showing the yellow or rusty-coloured iron that was exploited by Iron Age people. When the turf and heather is removed the upper layer of peat is reddish and crumbly. That is the Sphagnum peat. The lowest levels are black and solid, and it can be imagined that given sufficient time and pressure would become a something like coal. This is the fen peat. Tree stumps are found below the Sphagnum layer, and can be seen scattered about the peat diggings at Lindow today. Lindow Man lay near the junction of the Sphagnum and the Fen layers.

At Lindow the deepest peat found is 7.15 metres. But this is where peat diggers have already taken off about 3 metres. So the total depth was perhaps 10 metres, or more than 30 feet. This is unusually deep. Typically

Opposite: Abigail and Herbert Worsley in their 'own use' Eccups Lane moss room.
courtesy Eric Worsley

a peat bog would be between 2 and 5 metres deep.

In ancient times peat was a low-grade resource that was available to anyone who was prepared to dig it out. This became enshrined in law as the immemorial right of Turbary. In due course a method was found of sharing the peat lands out. Everybody had a patch of the bog somewhere, like an allotment, and would dig it for their own fuel. This is still the case in parts of Ireland. The patch is called a Moss Room, and because of the way it is demarcated it gradually becomes characteristically long and thin. 'What are called Moss Rooms are narrow plots of land on a peat bog, formerly allotted for turbary to each house in the township. Each person was restricted to width, but might work towards the centre of the moss as far as he liked. Consequently the moss rooms became in time long narrow strips. In many cases they have been drained, enclosed and cultivated; so that in the vicinity of the bog there are a number of very long and narrow fields.' Stephen Murray 1909

These long and narrow fields, the moss rooms, are very obvious on a big scale map. Good examples can be seen radiating from Paddock Hill towards Row of Trees. From Row of Trees and Upcast Lane Northwards. From Eccups Lane. And coming right into Wilmslow in the area now built up between Moor Lane and Strawberry Lane. The long thin Moss Rooms contrast markedly from ordinary fields and so define the edges of the Moss. At Row of Trees, for instance, there is ordinary farmland and hedgerows on the south side towards Chorley, but a totally different landscape on the north side, spongy underfoot with straight paths, silver birches and long narrow Moss Rooms.

People living in Lindow today still remember this way of working the peat. Eric Worsley, who was born in 1914 and lives still on Eccups lane, remembers:

"This is a photo of mother and father cutting turves on't moss. Putting the turves in windrows. Birds used to nest in the windrows, especially wagtails. They rented a piece off Traffords or Council. It was at the back, where tip is now. Everybody had a piece, rented to them. They were honest, it was like a club. You borrowed somebody else's can if you'd left yours at home. You took the heather off first. Baled the water out with a can. Grey turf on top. Black turf underneath for firelighters. Birch twigs for pea-sticks. Special spades made for the job - flattened out, with a side."

A Spitfire pranged near Eric Worsley's peat room. Soft landing, pilot walked away. No petrol left in it the next morning! Someone had spirited it away.

People with nowhere else to go built shacks on the moss rooms themselves, like allotment sheds, but to live in for at least part of the year. George Potts recalls a character called Piddypod, because he had big feet

- *"dead slow and stop"*, who had a shack on a little Moss Room on Newgate by the Tip. Some had only clod huts, not even made of wood, with no chimney. Lenny and Charlie Adshead lived in such a place. The door at the front was only an old sack, though they slept on an old door.

In the 1920s and 30s the shack dwellers were organised into a small business by Eddie Bailey. Turves of the black peat, which shrank and became light when they were dry, were dipped in waste oil in an old bath to make firelighters. They were sold round the streets of Manchester, as Mary Payne at Row of Trees House can remember.

The peat diggers used to go to the Long Bar or Long Tap for lunch. It is the dirt track called Sandy Lane behind the huge glass show-room, once cars, now designer clothes. Walter Munnerley: *"Peat diggers used to sit on the banking, hundreds of them. Brought bottles from the off licence on Altrincham Road - put bottles in the heather to cool them. They all had huts and a strip apiece. Black Donkey Alehouse was at the other end."*

In the 1950s a different pattern of peat digging and marketing was started independently by Cyril Bradley and Roy Kirkham. Cyril Bradley, of Strawberry Lane but then living on Newgate, was in the lawn turf business, but it was no good in times of drought or frost. He could not lay the men off, so he was looking for another line of business that would keep them in work.

Cyril used to go in the evenings with a spade and make exploratory digs in the fields which had not then been dug for peat. He knew from his friend, Jimmy Ellison, who worked in the council offices that test drilling had shown 30 feet of peat, followed by a clay barrier, then alabastine. So when Arthur Mountfield's holdings on Lindow came up for sale, which included fields on both sides of Rotherwood Road, he was ready. Braggins held the sale at the Royal Oak. It was all to be sold in small parcels, but Cyril hustled the sale, sending up the price and spoiling the auction (his words). Afterwards he spoke to Peter Gass and said *"What about the lot? What about £1000?"* He ended up paying £1200 for the lot.

First of all he made garden composts. Cyril Wood told Christine: *"At one time I was working for Cyril Bradley - he had a lawn turf business and he started peat shredding (past Ned Yates). We had to shred it, the brown peat, it was - mix it in something like a cement mixer with a tiny bit of fertiliser and some gritty sand. Sold it bagged as John Innes. Trouble was, he never dried the peat out - he was selling about 70% water!"*

The peat was all dug by hand. The men were paid 2/6 per yard (but they never were a yard says Alan Mould). Deep litter chicken farming was another use for the peat, and mushroom growing.

Meanwhile Roy Kirkham was carrying out a similar operation with a yard next to his bungalow on Moor Lane. His operation was called

Narrow gauge rail tracks running across the peat bog to the yard at Newgate.

Peat extraction in the 1960s: *"The peat was all dug by hand. The men were paid 2/6 per yard"*

Mow Cop peat diggers at Lindow Moss 1969
Left to right: Gerald Bibby, Frank Mould and Gordon Capeston
courtesy Cheshire County Council, Wilmslow Library

Trucking the peat c1965
Sydney Wheeler collection, courtesy Wilmslow Historical Society

Saltersley Common c1970. Day-wagers making a peat stack.
Alan Mould is in the wagon hurling the dried turves
courtesy Cheshire County Council, Wilmslow Library

Peat cutting machine 1960s
Sydney Wheeler collection, courtesy Wilmslow Historical Society

FINA PEAT. All hand digging until the 1960s, when Roy sold out to Fisons, who brought the mechanical diggers in. Fisons tried to bust Cyril by undercutting him to all his customers, pushing his turnover down to almost nothing. Then they offered him a silly buy-out, say £500.

Buxton Mushrooms saved the day. Cyril, thinking *'right, how can I wind up the business without giving in to them?'* went straight up to Harpur Hill near Buxton, where the mushroom-growing business was. By chance the two owners, from Wrington Vale Mushroom Farm, Churchill, Somerset, were there that day. Cyril put the case to them. Evidently persuasively. They offered him a £7000 buy-out plus a 5 year contract to supply to supply two lorry-loads of peat to Harpur Hill per day.

The peat was still dug by hand, during August - March, which was reasonably kind to the natural flora and fauna. Hay knife to slice it, spade to dig it out. They did try a German machine for a while, that cut the peat in blocks, but it never worked well at Lindow. Each piece was turned on its side then stacked at the side of the room. When the winds started in March each piece was turned again on its side, using hands because by now they were pretty light. They ended up with huge long banks of peat blocks. It was collected by a train on temporary tracks, pulled by a little sideways-sitting loco (which still exists, stored somewhere near Chinley. It was in Bruntwood Park for a while.) and taken to the depot which was on the corner of Newgate and Rotherwood next to the Humane Society.

Cyril was very impressed by the Harpur Hill operation. The mushrooms were grown in caves that had been used as bomb storage during the two world wars. They were huge, you could drive an 8-wheeler

Cyril Bradley's Newgate peat yard
Sydney Wheeler collection, courtesy Wilmslow Historical Society

right in. The mushrooms were grown in side caverns off the main drag. Eighteen wagons went out every morning to collect horse manure from racecourses and stables. It was mixed with spent grains from breweries, and sterilised. The mix was machine graded into perfect beds four inches deep. Then it was seeded with the mycelium, which was grain with a white fungal coating, sprinkled thinly. An inch of Lindow peat mixed with limestone chips was spread on the top. Then it was all left for six weeks or so in the dark and the warm to grow.

Every morning a fleet of buses brought in an army of girls to pick the mushrooms. They worked with lights like miner's lamps on their heads, picking 7 tons a day. Button mushrooms were picked first, then after a week's rest a second pick. Then the spent stuff was simply slung out on the fields. Cyril would have liked to bring it back on his lorries, mill it and sell it, but he was never allowed to for fear of circular infection.

All went well until the Harpur Hill operation was taken over by a firm called Country Kitchens, ex-Coal Board people, who had no idea how to run it. They decided to collect the raw peat from Lindow and dry it at the other end. Cyril enjoyed describing to us how their lorry was loaded up at Lindow under their instructions and sank immovably into the bog. It took three days to get it out.

Country Kitchens was in turn taken over by Heinz to safeguard their mushroom supply. Lindow Man was found during the Heinz era in 1984. Heinz also took over Roy Kirkham's business. Cyril's yard closed and all operations were concentrated at Roy Kirkham's yard on Moor Lane, as they are today.

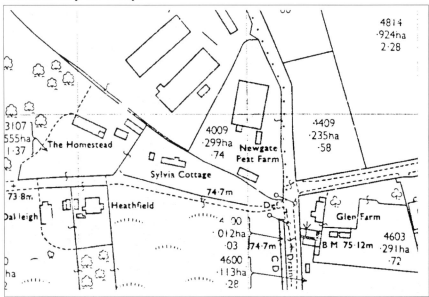

Map showing Cyril Bradley's yard at Newgate

Bruce Mould of Mow Cop tells the story from the peat digger's point of view. He started work in 1950 when he was 14. He worked on a farm when he first left school, with his mate Kenny Mellor, but they were worked to death. So he went to Eclipse at Alsager and was put to work on Alsager Moss on piece work. Kenny didn't take to it, but Bruce carried on, learning how to work it the best way. By 1959 he was earning £7.10s., well above the national average. Alsager Moss is at Radway Green; he travelled by bike, a 13 mile trip. When the peat was all gone there was white silica sand underneath it, which is being dug out in its turn today. Next he worked at Congleton Moss, between the A34 and the Macclesfield Road. That was dug out as well. Then for a time at Whixall Moss near Wem in Shropshire as well. Whixall has escaped the fate of the other peat bogs. In 1990 it was declared a nature reserve under English Nature and the Countryside Council for Wales. The hope is that enough is left for it to regenerate.

All the Mould family were peat diggers. The four brothers, Frank, Jim, Les and Bruce, would travel in an old van, or an old car - a beetle, or on motor bikes. The Mountford family, also from Mow Cop but on the Staffordshire side, were also peat diggers. Mow Cop was another marginal place, like the peat bogs, shunned by the comfortable classes. As a digression, we noticed that Bruce pronounces the name of his home Mow to rhyme with Cow, often leaving out the Cop. He pronounces his own surname Mowl to rhyme with Cowl. The rival family Mountford have the same sound, Mowntford. Which came first, the place name or the family name? And just how long has the family been there?

In the summer Bruce would start at four in the morning and be on his way home when other people were going out to work. His wife Betty and the children would sometimes come too during the school holidays. The kids didn't like turning the blocks to dry - too heavy - but they liked stacking it in pyramids.

He worked at Roy Kirkham's first, then left to go to Cyril's because he paid 6d more. There were about eighteen cutters then, under Fisons, all cutting by hand. They used an ordinary grafting spade, which they used to bend a bit more so it was easier on the back. Country Kitchens wanted to cut the workforce down. They brought in a machine, like you see in Ireland. It was a German machine, all worked by cams. Bruce went on a course and was taught

Roy Kirkham at Paddock Chase, following his retirement.
courtesy Cheshire County Council,

how to use it and look after it by the Germans. But it never worked well at Lindow because when it hit a buried tree stump everything was thrown out of adjustment. Bruce is a clever mechanic. He made a lot of the machinery at the yard, which tipped the railway wagons and elevated the peat to the top of the stack. His brother made the oak bodies of the wagons, with opening doors both sides. The footbridges near Saltersley, still in use, were made by Bruce.

He recalls the peat digging operations and seasons like this:
1. Cutting it in winter. You worked on your own, trying out different ways of doing it best. You dug it out in three spade-depths, like steps. It was in 66 yard compartments, not like the old moss rooms. One day in nine hours he went up 66 yards and down 66 yards - that's 132 yards. He reckons he must have dug 150 ton of peat that day - a record?
2. Stacking the turves in pyramids about 4 foot high in spring. Working in twos or whatever.
3. In July - stooking it. 5 or 6 pyramids went into one. Turn 'em round so dry side in.
4. August- stack it in lines 66 yards long, 14 or 15 feet high. Bloke on top maybe 2 below.
5. It was taken to the yard in the little train.
They took 4 layers off in the years he worked here, which is about 12 feet. That was from the lowest bit by Saltersley.

Bruce Mould finished peat digging in 1976. By then there were only the four brothers and Gordon and Syd Capeston left working, plus Ken, the manager from Harpur Hill. Bruce by then was in charge on the site. One Saturday he had let the men go off early once the work was done. By bad luck the area manager came round after they had all gone. So he got the sack. He does not seem very aggrieved about it.

What was it like digging the peat? It was hard work. In summer it was very hot. In frosty weather it all froze, all along side of the cut. You could just chop it off, which the others did, but Bruce covered his bit with straw the day before. You could make a beautiful fire though, out of the old roots (four thousand years old!). A ring of turves with the fire in the middle, or a tin drum with holes. One day a mate who was a miner, off the coal face, came down to see what he did for a living. His verdict: *"you buggers want a medal - a medal as big as a frying pan"*.

The mushroom-growing operation at Harpur Hill folded overnight when the law giving equal pay for women came in. Lindow peat is no longer dug by hand, nor is the little railway in operation. Twisted lengths of track lie about on the bog as forlorn and useless as the ancient tree stumps.

Today Lindow is being mechanically dug and air dried in situ by Croghan Peat of Somerset. The process is destructive of all wildlife, making a brown desert. *"I canna believe it, can you Bruce?"* said Betty Mould when they visited Lindow in 2002 after a 25 year absence. *"It isn't the same bog"* was his reply. The old yard on Moor Lane, where Lindow Man was found, is still in use; a mountain of loose peat and parking for a few machines. Bruce was excited to find a section of the old two-foot gauge track still in place at the back, with four of the little wagons that his brother had made, and the elevator machinery that he had made himself. *"I've enjoyed it, but its upsetting"* was his final verdict.　MH

When Bruce Met Cyril ....
Reunited for the first time in 30 years, Bruce Mould, left, and Cyril Bradley were delighted to see each other and had a long trip down memory lane.

Bruce Mould rediscovers four of the little wagons that his brother had made, and the elevator machinery that he had made himself in the 1960s.

"Young Barry longed to drive the main digger, that wonderful lime green Hy-Mac which rose powerful and dominant over the damaged landscape, cratering the ground as it sliced out gigantic slabs of peat ...."

Lindow End

Now lying rusting and abandoned in the peat farm yard.

One man and his ditch - Bruce Mould was surprised and delighted to discover one of the ditches he had excavated by hand over 30 years ago. It is still functioning in an abandoned area of the bog.

Hand peat diggers Bruce Mould and his nephew Alan on the bridge which crosses one of the main ditches. Most of the bridges on the peat bog were built by Bruce in the 1960s.

We were fortunate to learn of the existence of a short ciné film showing working life on the peat moss. Made by Cyril Bradley in the 1960s, it is an important historical record and the original now rests with the Northwest Film Archive.

The following selection of pictures have been extracted from the film and the quality is not always good. Some are rather blurred and fuzzy, but even so, we felt that they should be included in this book. Our thanks go to Cyril and also to the Northwest Film Archive.

PLATE 19.

13
Natural
History

Lizars sc.

1 & 2. *Black Arches, male & fem.*
3. *Scarlet Tiger-moth.* 4. *Var. of D°*

Natural History

Extracts From A Schoolboy's Nature Notebook 1932-34

Author Unknown

1932

1 January: Saw kestrel flying over the Riflemans Arms.

February: Newts on Lindow Common. Mole traps set by Mr Rigby at Prestons. Found Elephant Hawk Moth chrysalides

5 March: Several skylarks singing on the Common

13 March: Tawny Owls nesting.

18 March: Frogs laying spawn in large numbers on the Common. Also newts.

25 March: Found Rook's eggs

22 April: Bees and swallows on the Common.

23 April: Found an owls nest on Saltersley Common.

29 April: Tiger beetle: Linnets: Common lizard. Heard the cuckoo.

May: Found Peewit's nests on Lindow Common. Heath moths, wagtails, Yellowhammer's nest and a Green Hairstreak butterfly. In Saltersley Wood there were Turtle and Ring doves and a lark's nest. On the peat bog I found Reindeer Moss, a pheasant's nest, also linnets, whitethroats and redpolls. Also Fox moths, a large dragonfly, a Yellow Underwing and a lizard.

23 July: Permission from Mr Bailey to go into the wood at Saltersley. Saw a kestrel and found a linnet's nest with four eggs.

August: saw a small copper on Lindow.

1 October: Seagulls on the common.

18 December: Ice on Lindow. Lots of gulls.

Elephant Hawk moth

Opposite: Entomological plate of 1836 : British Moths

1933

3 February: The skylarks were singing on Saltersley today. The weather is mild and there are frogs in the pond a Lindow Common. Also saw a kestrel over the common.

19 February: A flock of fieldfares at Prestons, near the peat common.

10 April: Saw a goldfinch. He was quite tame. They are not so common as they used to be. Visited the Dragonfly Pond*. The main rookery is near Wilmslow station. The swans left Lindow today. They have been there since 23 March. Saw Green linnets.

*Green Lake, which dried up and gradually vanished in the 1950s, probably due to drainage of the peat bog. An early victim of peat extraction, it is now just an indentation in the ground.

6 May: In the afternoon I went to the peat common. Everywhere is very green and fresh and looking new. Heard the cuckoo. Saw lots of martins together. Also a shrike, a common lizard, linnets, thrushes, chaffinches, hedge sparrows, yellowhammers, reed buntings, willow warblers and winchats. Amongst the moths were Purple Hairstreaks, Buff tips and Cinnabar.

9 June: Found skylark's nest in the sand hills today.

12 June: Whilst I have been away several nests on the peat common and Saltersley have been either deserted or destroyed. All the eggs are broken or gone. Found the Oak eggar moth, eyed moth, Burnet moth and a Goldtail. There are Large Skipper butterflies at Saltersley. Found Emperor moth larvae on Lindow Common. There is a sand martin's nest in the old sandpit at Saltersley.

At this point our young author suddenly acquires a camera -

22 July 1933: I took a photograph of Mike Preston and our hut on Saltersley.

26 July: Took photo of the sand martins 10 days after hatching.

30 July: Visited peat common: Red Admirals, Coppers, Yellow Underwings, Emperors and also the Oak Egger moth.

Oak Egger moth

7 August: Found redpoll's nest with eggs. The wagtails all seem to have vanished. An old chap who works on the peat told me that there had been a young cuckoo in one of the wagtail's nests in a peat stack, and that it had flown the week before. It is about 3 weeks since I saw a fully grown cuckoo.

Emperor moth

11 August: Broom moth on Lindow. Black ant's nest and red ant's nest on Saltersley. Red Admirals on Lindow common. White Ermine larvae. Poplar Hawk moth ready to pupate. Watched it bury itself - it only took 5 minutes to completely disappear!

22 August: Baker took photograph of wagtail's nest in peat stack. Goldtail caterpillar in hedge.

31 August: Wilmslow is not like it used to be. Houses and estates are springing up everywhere and the commons are less wild and many trees are being cut down everywhere. Less is to be seen than formerly.

1 September: Bought stuffed merlin in a case for two shillings.

29 September: Kestrel over Lindow.

26 November: Shooting over Saltersley. Shot a snipe and a rook. Preston took the snipe home and cleaned and cooked it. Said it was very good. There are lots of snipe and wagtails around the sewage beds.

27 November: Saw heron mobbed by rooks.

2 December: We went across the fields near Gillibrand's farm today. Had fine view of a heron, which flew up from the little stream, which is lower than the field and hidden from view. The heron landed only a field away.

7 December: Frost and fog. Lindow Common is holding for skating.

Emperor Caterpillar

1934

20 January: Hawks Wood is being cut down. I asked a man who was getting wood and he said it would be cut down all the way to Bollin Farm. Many trees on Saltersley are being felled. Saw a Green woodpecker.

12 February: The local name for starling is shenster. I have not heard this before. First heard the skylark singing - 26 February 1932, 2 February 1933 and 12 February 1934. In Hawks Wood there are hazel catkins, palm and daisies. Saw a yellowhammer on Lindow common.

27 March: Saw a fox in Lesser Jay Wood at Saltersley - this is the first one I have seen alive.

21 April: Violets and primroses in Hawk Wood.

10 May: Blew a kestrel's egg for Miss Downes. It came from Saltersley.

12 May: Tawny Owls with chicks in Hawk Wood. Also a sparrow hawk.

2 June: Went to Hawk Wood but was turned out by a man I have not seen before.

3 June: Peat bog - wagtails, redpolls, blackbirds and linnets, all with young. Also saw a kingfisher and some Fox moths.

8 July: Green Emerald and Red Admiral at Tay Bridge (this was a small footbridge over the Bollin at the top of Dooleys Lane, Morley Green). Very hot. The lake on the common is terribly low. I have seen Brimstone butterflies, White Ermines, Black Arches, Silver Tips, Goldtail moths, Meadow Browns, Tortoishells and the larvae of Emperors and Buff Tips. There has been no sign of the Cream Spot Tigers since 1930.

Cream Spot Tiger moth

6 September: Greenfinches nest on the peat bog. Also many fieldfares eating rowan berries there. Went fishing in the pike pit at Lindow End and also the perch pit in Nine Acre field.

7 October: Shooting on the peat bog. Missed a cock pheasant. Temperature 60F. Lay in the grass.

14 October: Some excitement caused by our shooting on the peat last week. One old chap said "Ere, it'll be a summons if y'ere found out right enough. The Warden was 'ere just after you'd gone last week." Unknown we had caused quite a lot of excitement!

4 November: Borrowed Mr Rigby's ferret and we had a good ratting in Mike's (Prestons) loft. Micky (the dog) is a fine ratter. Rex is learning and shows promise. On the vermin poles at Redesmere we counted over 100 animals and birds.

Pathway to the peat bog

Regenerating vegetation at Whixall Moss, Shropshire, now a nature reserve. 2002

An abundance of regenerating vegetation at Springfield, Newgate. Many rare species of tiny mosses and ferns flourish here, undisturbed.

"The purple heather blooms on Lindow in the autumn and in the season whinberries are plentiful. From some parts of Mobberley the hill of Alderley Edge can be seen in bold outline.There is plenty of game in the Mobberley fields. Rabbits are numerous on some of the farms, and hares and partridge may often be seen. Hedgehogs seem to find a suitable home and moles are fairly plentiful, according to report. Birds are everywhere and fill the air with song. Crab apple trees stand in many hedgerows in which can be found the wild raspberry, whilst every lane in summer time is bright with wild flowers and butterflies." Stephan Murray 1909

The Moulds are a well known family of traditional peat cutters from Mow Cop. Starting at the age of fifteen, Bruce Mould spent the whole of his working life 'on the peat', much of it on piece work at Lindow. He was there for 25 years, from the 1950s-1970s, together with other family members. They all travelled down from Mow Cop together, arriving at 4am in the summer months and working through until 2pm. Alan Mould, Bruce's nephew, remembers it well.

"It was magic at 4am - we cared, we did it gently, not like today. We took the top turf off, dug the peat to 3 feet, then replaced the top turf as we went down the trench."

Now in his late seventies Bruce Mould came back to see the bog with his wife, Betty. They were both shocked. Bruce was visibly upset. *"Oh God, what have they done to it? It's a dead thing. Betty and the kids used to come back here with me after school, to turn the turves. The kids loved it. They used to find lizards and newts. All the birds were singing."*

This was in the same week that we had visited Whixall Moss in Shropshire, and had seen what can be achieved after ten years of careful management to rescue and revive.

7 May 2002: Matthew and I saw a large green woodpecker in the field between Newgate and Greaves Road. A sulphurous green woodpecker cunningly designed to blend with the powdery algae that covers the branches of all the old tall trees. It stayed for a long time and appeared to be ground feeding, having found an ant's nest in the grass.

Later we heard another woodpecker, this time a greater spotted, apparently drilling INSIDE a large tree on the bridle path just in front of Lindow House, off the Racecourse Road end of Newgate. On the ground beneath the tree, a lot of tiny new wood fragments were scattered like sawdust. It may have a nest inside the trunk. There seem to be plenty of greater spotteds in the area

27 July 2002: Walked to Saltersley Common to photograph the sundews in flower - the last little pockets of resistance, but not for much longer.

They are already as rare there as lark's nests. I found the tiny sundews, *Drosera rotundifolia*, flowering bravely amongst the exposed remnants of the primeval forest graveyard, awaiting the approach of the excavator. They will not have to wait long; the latest tyre tracks are only about three feet away. Monday morning? Sad to know that this will be their final flowering.

The airport is busy with holiday traffic - planes are rising into the skies above the moss incessantly, whilst far below I watch more ancient fight paths, those of the creatures born to fly. There are hardly any birds here, but a few feet above ground level I encounter lots of dragonflies - yellow four spotted chasers. Also Brimstone butterflies, the Large heath butterfly, and Cinnabar moths. A peculiar looking spider hangs suspended from its silken skein on a large bush of common heather. Some fluffs of cotton grass, bulrushes about to turn to brown velvet and sedge rushes now in full flower. A tall riot of wild flowers - foxgloves, bright yellow shepherds purse and purple vetch, rebelling still on the fringe of Fir Wood.

Many people have told me about the lizards and the great crested newts which they remembered from their childhood days. Both species have disappeared. Tomorrow is International Bog Day, marking the ongoing reclamation and restoration of wetlands and bogs across the globe. But at Lindow there is nothing to celebrate.

I live a few minutes walk away from the peat bog and yes, there is a constant turf war between my lawn and the various mosses. I don't kill the moss, just gentle discouragement by way of constant mowing, aerating and scarifying. Sometimes, in a dry spell, I almost think that I have won. I delude myself. I have tried to make the garden attractive to wildlife and have been pleasantly surprised by the wide range of visitors who arrive to join the many resident frogs, wood mice, shrews, insects and moths. Maybe they come because the bog is laid bare, a sterile, dead thing, and their habitats are destroyed.

Regular garden callers include foxes and cubs - I spoil them with cat food scraps. They live in the woods around the peat bog, pretty much undisturbed. In the Iron Age the fox was a revered animal. Nobody ate foxes. The Celtic leader Lovernius was named after the fox. The fox disappears into its earth so the Celts may have believed that this animal had powerful links with the Otherworld, the abode of their ancestors. It may be fanciful to think that my foxy visitors could be the descendants of that very same Celtic fox which provided the fox fur arm band that Lindow Man was wearing when he was sacrificed, but the idea rather pleases me.

The sparrowhawk sometimes visits my garden and sits on top of the walkway arbour, swivelling his head in all directions in search of prey. He sometimes stays for about twenty minutes and once left a squirrel petrified, quite literally, for a good ten minutes after swooping towards him as the squirrel was stealing peanuts from the bird feeder. There are lots of finches; bullfinch, chaffinch, greenfinch and goldfinch, nuthatches, tree creepers, and long tailed tits. Thrushes and blackbirds, jay, wood pigeon and collared doves. Occasional seasonal visitors include redstarts, a heron, a weasel and, just once, a polecat!

This was at 7pm on Sunday 17 December 2000: I was ready to go to a Carol Service and turned on the outside light to look for the cats. I saw something large at the far end of the garden, moving towards the house, then Oscar-cat wondering whether to chase it. He started to follow it stealthily. It came closer, with a raised back which gave it a strange lurching, hobbled gait. As it meandered into the light I thought my eyes were deceiving me. Cream and black, ferret shaped, but much larger, it was unmistakably a polecat. Oscar, territorial to the point of lunacy, chased it under the fence into next door's garden. I have never seen it since and had assumed that it was someone's exotic pet, possibly escaped from the kennels across the fields whilst being boarded for the Christmas period. I checked the natural history book. Yes, definitely a polecat. I received some old fashioned looks of disbelief when I recounted this tale.

It was not until we recently visited Whixall Moss near Wem, in Shropshire, to see their ten year reclamation project for ourselves that I did a rethink. There the polecat is listed as one of their native bog mammals and is flourishing once more on Whixall Moss.

Perhaps all these creatures, deprived of their natural habitats, have moved closer towards the gardens. But there are no longer corncrakes, skylarks or grey wagtails. Partridge and curlew are also gone. Large scale commercial peat extraction, crop spraying, runways and new golf courses have all spelt disaster for the ground nesting birds.

Howard, a friend, was brave enough to recount to me a tale of the 1960s. I'm sure that he, too, must have been the recipient of disbelieving looks when he told people: *"It was winter time, growing dusk and I was walking the dog up Rotherwood Road like I always did. I must have been about eleven years old. The dog was off his lead and he ran onto the bog, so I went after him. Suddenly I felt I was being watched. I looked around, nothing. Then I looked up. The bare branches were full of eyes. Owls - dozens of them, all gathered in the trees, staring down at me. I stopped counting them when I reached twenty. I was really spooked. I ran back to the road and waited for the dog. The really queer thing was that the owls were all different sorts."*

Jenny Nixon has lived at Coppock House for twelve years. The house is Victorian and of nice proportions but the barns and outbuildings

Stella Willett enjoying her small Nature Reserve at Saltersley, a much needed oasis for the bog flora and fauna whose habitats have been destroyed by ongoing peat extraction

A fox in my garden. Unable to hunt due to an injured hind leg, this young fox arrived at 10am one July morning, driven by hunger. He survived and now has a slight limp.

courtesy Mark Heslop

are older, dating from the 18th century. One of the barns has been reduced in size by about one third. It has great, impressive beams.

Originally a farm, much of the surrounding land was sold off by the previous owners to make way for the Mobberley golf course, which now encroaches all their perimeters, so that they are surrounded by golfers. The course opened 1995-96. Jenny feels that the golf club has failed to comply with its original 'green' obligations, as promised. They have, for example, taken out entire ancient hedgerows instead of just making a passage through, as agreed. The regular spraying of weed killer has caused the Coppock boundaries to suffer from wind-born spray and all the wild hedgerow flowers have been destroyed.

Jenny recalls one of the worst days, when the ongoing construction of the golf course destroyed a large field of nesting curlews. Eggs smashed, for the entire day the air was filled with their grief stricken cries as the bereaved birds gathered nearby. Then the curlews left, and have never returned. So have the hares. All that remains is a multitude of rabbits. There is constant mowing, golf balls everywhere, privacy spoilt. The construction of the golf course has caused irreparable damage to the countryside. Some of the ancient tracks and pathways, which for centuries must have connected to Saltersley, are gone forever, disappeared under the greens.

Coppock House is surprisingly close to the edge of the peat bog. The sand hills are only two fields away, and one can stand and watch the mechanical peat digger in operation. The next farm, Hollingee, is within hailing distance of Coppock House and their land runs straight onto the bog.

Wild flowers and herbs continue to flourish undisturbed in the hedgerows around Hard Hill, at the top of Moor Lane. In summertime the old green lanes where the Gypsies used to roam are still *"bright with wild flowers and butterflies"*. Dog roses, cow parsley, vetch and campion, valerian and wild honeysuckle. Purple foxgloves and white convolvolus wend through the hawthorn bushes.

Once virtually undisturbed apart from the more gentle householder turbary, the rare *Ledum palustre* - the Labrador tea shrub - once grew all over the bog. It was a vital ingredient in Gypsy herbal medicine. Today only one fine specimen survives, its location a closely guarded secret. In spring and summer months it is covered in umbels of creamy white flowers which glow in the dusk of evening and later, in the blackness of the night, gleaming pallidly amidst the dark nocturnal life of the bog it becomes a ghostly wraith.

CP

14
The March of
Progress?

The March Of Progress?

A 3RD RUNWAY FOR RINGWAY? Government Air Service
Study identifies the potential of a third runway
and fourth terminal at Ringway.

Macclesfield Times August 1, 2002

Lindow Moss is even today a remarkably peaceful and attractive place. It
sometimes feels as though it is in some way out of this world. But it is not.
The 21st century is very close.

The peace is disturbed at frequent intervals by a plane for Marbella
or Frankfurt taking off startlingly close by. The runway is only just
beyond the north west border of the bog.

When a bog cottage is sold the price makes one gasp and stretch
one's eyes. It will inevitably be transformed, as so many have done
already, into an SK9 residence with black 4WDs outside. At the Wilmslow
end parts of the bog are already solidly built over. So Lindow Moss is
under threat from both directions. In the 1930s Lindow was seen as an
undesirable place, inhabited only by unimportant people. This made it
vulnerable, on the NIMBY principle, to a different threat.

The Tip

Peat bogs are typically perceived as places to be shunned by decent folk.
That is why in times of trouble they are a refuge for the persecuted, and
why even up to our own time they are home to misfits, people who could
not fit in anywhere else.

Faced with the ever-growing problem of rubbish and where to tip
it, Councils often turn their eye to such a place. Lindow Tip started in
about 1933. Jack Barratt, who was a gardener at Pownall Hall, levelled the
land for the Council. The Council made up Newgate from a typical
Lindow trackway into a proper road. The rubbish was brought in little
waggons with half-barrel-shaped backs with sliding lids. Thousands and
thousands of tons of best peat are buried under there, as Eric Worsley told
us, unbelievingly.

During the war years aircraft wrecks were brought down here by
the lorries called Queen Marys. They were stacked 3 and 4 deep;
Whitleys, Wellingtons, gun turrets, wings. Walter Munnerley remembers
playing there as a boy and pinching perspex to make rings and suchlike.
It was separated from the main Newgate tip. After the war they all
disappeared very quickly. There is a big bungalow standing there now, by
Ned Yates's Garden Centre.

Opposite: 1997. Under siege from above and below, protesters took to the trees.

The council tip here is closed now, unlike the mountainous one on Dane's Moss near Macclesfield, but who knows when pressure of circumstances might induce the Council to re-open it? The rubbish pile was sealed over to make a sort of artificial Downland, dry and limestony, raised high above the bog, densely planted with sapling trees. It is not an unpleasant place but it is completely alien. Two or three burners, like silver mushrooms in their wire enclosures, waste day and night the methane that is being generated by the festering rubbish underneath; a constant reminder of its origin.

Pluto

It is an acronym. The initials stand for Pipe Line Under The Ocean. All the locals who are old enough remember it, people keep talking about it, but it is hard to find facts. PLUTO was built in preparation for D-Day in 1944, to get fuel over to the Normandy beaches for the invading armies. The under-the-ocean bit was under the English Channel. The section across Lindow Moss was part of a link between Ellesmere Port and the depot and sidings at Poynton. Its name must have been a puzzle to many. Each section was done by a different contractor. Taylor Woodrow did the Lindow section. It is made of 6" iron pipes bolted together in lengths and buried, its course marked at intervals by a white painted hurdle. When it was no longer useful it was flooded with seawater. It is not buried very deep and occasionally bits get dug up, as Barbara and Kenneth Howe did at Springfield on Newgate when making a pond. The dug up sections lie in a stack nearby.

The Airport

The second Runway of Manchester Airport, opened on 7/8 February 2001, does not encroach on Lindow but it is so close that we thought it should be part of this book.

The original Ringway site was bought by Manchester in 1935 and the airport opened three years later. It was Britain's first Municipally-owned aerodrome. Only a year after opening it was overtaken by the war, although it was never requisitioned. In 1940 it was selected for training men in a new and untried form of warfare - parachute drops. They carried out their training drops in Tatton Park, where a rough stone monument near the Old Hall remembers them. In Terminal 1 a coloured glass screen, now in the chapel, is their memorial. The airport grew prodigiously during the war years, with three new tarmac runways, ten new hangars, and many other military buildings. All this gave the airport a flying start when war ended. The 1945 City of Manchester Plan predicted that the airport would be as important to the city as the Ship Canal had been in its day.

In 1962 a new terminal and control tower, now called T1, were built in place of the old 1930s Deco ones. The new buildings were lined up along the old Ringway Road, which although it has disappeared thus determines the geometry of the whole airport. The old country road is still there in fossil form at the foot of the Terminal buildings on the Air Side, a curious survival that will amuse some future archaeologist.

Ringway Airport has grown continuously since it started and is now the third largest in the country. As Manchester International Airport (how soon before it is renamed David Beckham Airport?) it is the city's flagship, its big earner and its big spender. It is in fierce competition with Liverpool, with West Midlands and Edinburgh, and with the London Airports.

The Second Runway

Is it necessary? Is it safe? It was on the cards for twenty-five years. Air traffic consultants pushed for it, safety officers worried about it, Cheshire Councils and the National Trust hired lawyers to fight it, Eco-warriors lay in front of bulldozers to resist it, or would have done if they had not been evicted from their tunnels and trees first. Reams of paper were covered in dense argument, huge doorstep-like documents lie well-thumbed but forgotten now in libraries. In the end there were only two possible outcomes, yes or no. And being realistic or fatalistic, which many were before even the first sod was turned, only one. Runway two is built. Most of us have used it, as we realise when the plane crosses Runway 1 or when, peering out of the tiny holes of scratchy perspex that planes have for windows, we glimpse the verdant Bollin woods. Moments after takeoff we are over Tatton Park, less than the length of the runway away.

The following is included as a personal historical record of the events leading up to the building of the second runway.

'*Come to these events!*', it says on a cheap pink news-sheet called 'RESIST RUNWAY TWO!' that I have kept since 1997. '*Sunday 6th April Guided runway walk with camp visit.*'

So I did. This was when the resistance was at its height. It was a long walk from the Ship Inn at Styal along the Bollin to Valley Lodge Hotel, across the road and up into the protest area which now, for it was all in vain, is under Runway 2, and then back via Bank House Farm and the packhorse bridge by Styal Mill. This is what I wrote on that day:

"About 30 people came led by Lance and there were other experts. V. mixed bag of people incl. 2 or 3 older than me, several foreign (French, Belgian, Irish) and several dogs. Beautiful country all the way. I had no idea it was so fine. Sheets of wood anemone, carpets of wild garlic not out yet. The whole idea of filling in the Bollin, with thousands of tons of the Peak District what's more, is grotesque.

An etching by Theo Olive evoking the mood of the protest.

From the Vantage Point you can see all the protesters' tree houses and also the police Range Rovers and the security men with their Landrovers and banks of lights. There's lots of fences going up - only one way into the site and that is guarded and gated. So we are only here on sufferance. There are 5 or 6 camps, each of them partly in the trees and partly underground. Trees are linked with pairs of blue walking ropes. They've built a bridge over the Bollin too. Very hard to know how many protesters are there. Maybe 50? There are little tent cities, with yurts made of branches with tarpaulins over them. Bits of brave festivity with flags and ribbons and arches of branches. 'Cliff Richard' is a camp built into the cliff of the Bollin with a couple of tree houses overhead. 'Sion Tree' is in and around a particularly fine Beech. Piles of dug-out earth and beaten path with the anemones flowering in between and the leaves just popping. Talked to several of the diggers tho' others kept up their trees and in their holes. The Security men are just boys in yellow flak jackets guarding lengths of fence and sometimes talking to the protesters. They have trained a bank of 6 lights pointblank on one of the tree houses. Two Range Rovers-worth of police zoomed up to see us off the premises."

The occupation lasted from spring into September 1997, ending with a four week battle and 230 arrests. Terry Waite and Martin Bell MP joined residents and protesters for a last march through on July 13th.

In 1976 local farmers joined the Action Group at Styal to protest against the extension of Runway 1.
courtesy Cheshire County Council, Wilmslow Library

Left: 1997 Runway 2 protesters gathered at a huge camp in the Bollin Valley, living in tree houses and underground tunnels. Local residents and shopkeepers showed their support, keeping them supplied with groceries.

Bollin Valley protest camp April 1997

The protesters built a makeshift bridge across the River Bollin ....

...... now diverted through this massive long tunnel which supports the second runway.

Hill House and Hanson House

When the second runway cut its swathe across Cheshire these two houses were in the way. They stood very close to each other on Wood Lane. Christine writes:

"Wood Lane was a typical winding Cheshire lane where we used to hack the horses. I remember we passed by a lovely old black and white house on a slight rise. The house was framed by trees and a lot of climbers - roses, wisteria, that sort of thing, very old fashioned English, pretty in summer. Tiny latticed windows, leaf framed gables.

The land fell away gently. There was a grassed embankment carpeted with crocus and snowdrops in early spring. The gardens were beautiful. There was a pool at the lowest point, with overhanging willows. This must have been the tanning pit originally. Despite the chocolate box image Hill House always looked confidently reassuring, snug and tranquil, part of the landscape. Hanson House was close by, but not so visible, almost opposite to Hill House. Just a glimpse of black and white through the trees."

They had to go, but as part of the Airport's £17M 'conscience budget' it was decided to move them and rebuild them somewhere else. Easier said than done, when you are dealing with an old rambling house that has been modified and codged up over the centuries. And where do you find a good enough new site? Practical considerations come in too. The original houses are not big enough, they don't have designer kitchens or enough bathrooms. Also the state of the original materials has to be taken account of. Which was bad.

Alan and Judy Lane of Hill House were the last people to leave, in August 1997. Before the houses were taken down the Archaeology Unit at the University did detailed surveys, right down to the individual pieces of wood and their peg holes. They recommended that the same firm did the demolition as did the re-erecting. That they should be hand dismantled and rebuilt. And that the processes of demolition and rebuilding should be simultaneous. This was not to be.

They were knocked down by a tough demolition man. At the end of that dreadful day he stood at the bar of the nearest pub in tears and announced sadly, *"In all the years I've worked on demolition I never ever thought I'd have to go through a day like this."*

The timbers, numbered with coded tags, were put into store in an old turkey shed along with the stone roofing flags and the plinth stones.

Now they are built anew. They are no longer close together. Hill House is on Nursery Lane at Soss Moss. Hanson House is out at Moss Lane, Siddington. Interesting that they should both end up on bog land sites. We have examined them both. Inevitably they are 2002 buildings, new houses on new sites but incorporating some pieces of the old houses and some elements of their design and plan. The new houses take their cue from the Cheshire style of the old, being genuinely timber-framed in oak with some decoration in the Cheshire mode. The sour smell of the tannins in the new wood was very strong. Many of the old timbers lay discarded on the grass outside, too rotten to use. The joiner told us that he and his father once lifted up a piece by its ends, but the middle stayed on the ground. The new timber is machine-sawn, and will not be not painted black but left to go gradually silver-grey. The infill panels are not wattle and daub either, and are painted ochre not white. The current fashion.

Hanson House now stands on a flat and windswept site, unattractive on a wet day. The flat dormers, without a cove, look wrong. It has old tile roofs and a stone plinth. The size of the house has been doubled by the simple expedient of building a completely new house behind and linking it to the rebuilt old one by a corridor and porch. I couldn't make any sense of the plan of the old house, it seemed like just a mishmash, until .... until I found the original door position, now blocked and only revealed by the slightly arched timber of its head. Then Bingo! It all falls into place. The door opened against the side of the fireplace, so you can not go straight in but have to turn right or left. You are baffled. It is a standard Cheshire plan, called a baffle entry house. The fireplace has been rebuilt, no doubt on valid evidence, as a timber-framed smoke hood. Inside the hood is a brass plate bearing the legend:

THIS SMOKE HOOD IS A HISTORIC FEATURE AND IS NOT TO BE
USED IN ANY CIRCUMSTANCES.

Hill House now is near the beautiful old Soss Moss Hall, but with the West Coast main line railway in between. Another flat site but the wood at the back gives some shelter. It is more attractive than Hanson House, because of its more comprehensible shape, coved dormers, fancy gables and stone flag roof. The date and initials 1620 RR can still be seen on a bressumer at the rear, but really it is a repro piece with old bits.

We walked as close to the original site of Hill House and Hanson House as possible on 27th February 2002. It is a chastening experience. The place simply does not exist any more. Christine's description might as well be pure fiction. Instead there is a long slog through squelchy clay round the seemingly endless windswept perimeter fence. The lane is cut off between Orrell House and Yarwood, the little Sugar Brook disappears into a heavily barred culvert. In between is an extraordinary dead centre, a no mans land, part of the world's air space but no longer part of Cheshire. Most planes taking off used less than half of the new runway - it was a windy day - but a Jumbo cargo plane lifted off with an effort only right at the end. From one point the terminal buildings could be seen, far away across the tarmac.   MH

Lady Lane, Mobberley, with Hill House in the background. Now vanished beneath the second runway.

Hill House c1880

courtesy Judy and Alan Lane

Hill House in its heyday - front aspect.

courtesy Judy and Alan Lane

The new Hill House taking shape, 2002

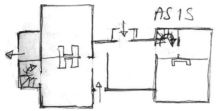

AS IS

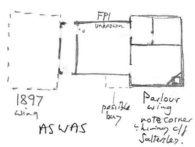

FP1
Unknown

1897
wing

possible
bay

Parlour
wing
note corner
chimney c/f
Saltersley.

AS WAS

HILL HOUSE Project

Detail of the on site reconstruction
work of Hill House, March 2002.

Hanson House 2002, showing the
door position and chimney in line,
indicating a baffle entry.

Hanson House rebuilt on a new site at Siddington, 2002.

Ancient Trackways And The Preservation Of Footpaths

I would like to make a gentle plea on behalf of our footpaths. Many now end abruptly, having been deliberately interrupted by land owners and householders to discourage walkers, so that over the years their original courses are lost forever. It is done using sly tactics - a gradual narrowing until the way is virtually impassable, the tipping of garden waste or landfill rubble so that it is blocked completely. Some have been religiously mown, so that they take on the appearance of lawn or extensions of the verges. I found one so narrow that is just a token now, lying between an overgrown hedge and a fence. Sideways passage by a small child is barely possible. Very soon it will be extinguished completely by lack of use. The worst offence I have seen is in the Gore Lane area, where the huge trunks of an ancient hedge have been savagely slashed to pieces in order to accommodate tall and ugly fencing panels.

In Warford I watched a puzzled rambler, staring up at a green bower and consulting her map. Ivy has been trained to grow up the post and obliterate the official sign. One day I may go there and cut it away, if no one else does.

It is enough that most of the land has vanished beneath the tarmac and concrete of our roads and towns, and that many old trackways have already been annihilated by runways and golf courses, without further encroachment by the unthinking householder.

Pathways that have been there for far longer than the properties are disappearing, as people deliberately try to eradicate these markers of the past. Many of the tracks are older than the written word, ancient rights of passage, messages stamped across the landscape by centuries of footsteps. Their destruction is gradually erasing our rural history.

The Future

Meteorological records only cover the last 350 years. Within their strata the peat bogs contain a complete table of the climatic changes which have taken place from pre-history to the present day. Their acidic conditions preserve evidence of past environments and store records which can be tracked back through 8000 years. Each strata is a living archive, and includes every fluctuation in the water levels, information which is vital and very relevant to current debates on global warming. Core samples extracted from peat bogs present paleontologists with the opportunity to study climatic variations throughout history. This supplies a basis for comparison against the more recent, human induced, changes which are principally due to the impact of the industrial revolution. Large scale mechanised cutting and draining of peat bogs in recent decades has altered or destroyed much of this important evidence.

Wetlands are important habitats for birds, plants and insects. They help to control flooding. They reduce pollution by storing carbon, thus regulating gas emissions and helping to alleviate the greenhouse effect. Peat bogs play an important role as nett 'fixers' of carbon. Peat is estimated globally to store 500 billion tonnes of carbon, therefore the ongoing extraction of peat for horticultural purposes has serious implications for global warming.

Drainage and consequent lowering of the water table poses a serious threat to the preservation of the archaeology which is preserved within the bogs. These include ancient timber trackways, artefacts, preserved bodies and the prehistoric forests which offer up their trees for dendrochronology. Despite their significant ecological role, wetlands are the least respected and most seriously abused of all environmental assets.

English Heritage have initiated a national strategy for wetland management, the MAREW (Monuments at Risk in England's Wetlands) project, which works closely with two other bodies, AHAP (Areas of High Archaeological Potential) and WARP (Wetlands Archaeology Research Project).

Unfortunately for Lindow's peat bog, the mineral rights which were granted by Macclesfield Borough Council are not due to expire until 21 February 2042. These rights were taken over by Somerset based Croghan Peat in May 1997. By 1999 the new company was submitting planning applications for the development of 60-90 houses on the site.

At this juncture the Saltersley Common Preservation Society was formed and in August 2000 Croghan Peat withdrew its application, on the understanding that a further revised application would be made. No doubt this will arrive in due course. In the meantime the peat continues to be extracted from an ever wider area. It is surface milled and transported by road to Somerset. Following a series of professional analyses commissioned at their own expense, the Saltersley Common Preservation Society concluded that the value of the extracted peat was £6-8 per cubic metre and the cost of extraction plus transport to Somerset was £13.50 per cubic metre. Mr Micawber would be predicting misery.

There are also great concerns regarding to the adverse effects upon the water table created by ongoing extraction. The main drainage ditches connect into Sugar Brook. There have been reports of flooded cellars, flooded fields and flooded gardens within the immediate vicinity. In addition there are flooding problems on the Lindfield Estate, hastily built in the 1920-30s to house those living in such sub-standard accommodation that local authority health and safety departments were obliged to intervene. Much of the estate stands on an area of original peat bog after the pools, clearly marked on the early maps, were drained.

Many of the poor families who lived around the bog were moved to Lindfield Estate. Some of them now have to don Wellingtons in order to enter their back gardens.

Lindfield estate, Wilmslow

Proposals for future restoration of the site, following cessation in 2042, include infilling by tipping over a 22 year period, commencing 20-30 years hence. Croghan Peat do not yet know what will be tipped but have indicated that it will take one of three forms - inert, non-inert or a mixture of the two. So what will be the votive offerings of the 21st century?

To save the bog would require the immediate cessation of peat extraction and the blocking up of the man made drainage channels to restore the water table to its original, natural levels. Only then would the bog plant seeds, rushes and moss spores have a chance to recolonise, encouraging the gradual return of the native flora together with the accompanying insect, bird, and animal life.

We will never see it as a raised peat bog during our lifetimes, but within ten years the site would be flourishing once more. It has been done at Fenn's, Whixall, Bettisfield, Wem and Cadney Mosses, where English Nature joined forces with The Countryside Council of Wales and stepped in to save Britain's third largest raised bog.

The reclaimed moss is now managed by English Nature and The Countryside Council of Wales as a National Nature Reserve, and is considered one of the gems of British wildlife. *"A surviving depth of one metre of peat is sufficient. From this it can be regenerated."* says Dr Joan Daniels, English Nature's site manager at Whixall.

What remains of Lindow Moss, the peat bog and the flora and fauna it has supported for thousands of years, is now in its final death throes. It is dying from dessication. We have tried to record something of its history and its people before everything is completely lost.

Bog pool

BIBLIOGRAPHY

A great deal has been written about Lindow man in particular, bog bodies as a group, and body preservation, human sacrifice, and pagan religion in general. We did not think it necessary to rehearse all the arguments here, so a brief list of further reading is appended.

Glob P V   The Bog People.   Faber&Faber 1969
This is the classic and beautiful book about bog bodies in Denmark that gave Lindow Man a meaning as soon as he turned up.
Stead, I.M., Bourke J.B. & Brothwell, Don (eds)
                              Lindow Man, the body in the bog.   BM 1986
The finding of Lindow man and the immediate discoveries about his mode of death.
Brothwell, Don 1986   The Bog Man   B M 1986
Ross, Anne & Robins, Don   The Life and Death of a Druid Prince.   Rider 1989
Attempts to give Lindow Man an identity and special significance.
Chamberlain, A.T., Pearson, M.P.Earthly Remains   BM 2001
Turner, R.C. & Scaife, R.G. (eds) Bog Bodies   BM 2002
Green M.A.   Dying for the Gods   Tempus 2001
More recent scientific evidence on Lindow man, and a full account of Lindow III.
Berry, Andre Q., Gale, Fiona, Daniels, Joan and Allmark, Bill (eds) 1996
                              Fenn's and Whixall Mosses   English Nature 2002

Sources of Reference
Squire   Celtic Myth and Legend   Gresham c1910
Ashe   King Arthur's Avalon   Collins 1957
Ross   Everyday Life of the Pagan Celts   Batsford 1970
Opie & Tatem (Ed)   Dictionary of Superstitions   OUP 1989
Watkins Alfred   The Old Straight Track   1925
Murray Stephan   History of Mobberley   Unpublished 1909
Fletcher Moss   Pilgrimages I &II   1901, 1903
Pearson Andrew   Wilmslow Past & Present   1897
Pemberton Christine Lindow End   Rex Publishing 2001
Hodson Howard   The Story of Wilmslow   1971
Mobberley WI   A History of Mobberley Village   John Sherratt 1952

Christine Pemberton lives on the fringes of Lindow Moss and knows the area well. With a long standing interest in the peat bog, which she has always found intriguing, she is concerned about the threat posed to its future survival by the ongoing extraction of peat.

Daughter of a Stockport bookseller, Christine has spent most of her working life within the book trade, including three years in Rome, with the publishing house of Feltrinelli.

Following some years as a features writer for a Staffordshire-based group of newspapers, she worked in the editorial department of a local history publisher, and has been involved in the production of many publications recording the histories of Staffordshire, Cheshire and Derbyshire. Her interests include walking, wildlife and landscape history.

Previous publications:-
Born to Win - the Story of Red Rum   Hodder & Stoughton 1979
Lindow End   Rex Publishing 2001